ETHICS IN THE THOUGHT OF EDWARD JOHN CARNELL

Kenneth W.M. Wozniak

WIPF & STOCK · Eugene, Oregon

Wipf and Stock Publishers
199 W 8th Ave, Suite 3
Eugene, OR 97401

Ethics in the Thought of Edward John Carnell
By Wozniak, Kenneth W. M.
Copyright©1983 by Wozniak, Kenneth W. M.
ISBN 13: 978-1-5326-8379-4
Publication date 3/4/2019
Previously published by University Press of America, 1983

To my wife
Ann
whose love and ethical sensitivity
are an unending source of
encouragement and inspiration

ACKNOWLEDGEMENTS

Acknowledgement is made to the following publishers and individuals for permission to quote from copyrighted material:

To Shirley Carnell Duvall for permission to quote from *The Theology of Reinhold Niebuhr* copyright (c) Eerdmans, 1960; *Television--Servant or Master?* copyright (c) Eerdmans, 1950; *An Introduction to Christian Apologetics* copyright (c) Eerdmans, 1948; and *A Philosophy of the Christian Religion* copyright (c) Eerdmans 1960.

To Timothy L. Smith, for permission to quote from *Revivalism and Social Reform* copyright (c) The Johns Hopkins University Press, 1980.

Quotations from *The Nature and Destiny of Man*, Volume II, by Reinhold Niebuhr, are reprinted with the permission of Charles Scribner's Sons, copyright (c) 1943, 1949, Charles Scribner's Sons, copyright renewed 1971, 1977.

Quotations from *The Burden of Soren Kierkegaard*, by Edward John Carnell, used by permission of William B. Eerdmans Publishing Co., copyright (c) 1965.

Quotes from "Should a Christian Go to War?" by Edward John Carnell (April 1951) reprinted by permission from HIS, student magazine of Inter-Varsity Christian Fellowship, (c) 1951.

Reprinted with permission of Macmillan Publishing Company, quotes from *Christian Commitment: An Apologetic* by Edward John Carnell, (c) Edward John Carnell 1957.

To Princeton University Press for permission to quote from Soren Kierkegaard, *Concluding Unscientific Postscript*, trans. David F. Swenson and Walter Lowrie. Copyright 1941 (c) 1969 by Princeton University Press.

Quotes from *The Case For Orthodox Theology*, by Edward John Carnell. (c) W. L. Jenkins MCMLIX. Used by permission of The Westminster Press.

v

TABLE OF CONTENTS

INTRODUCTION ix

    I   EDWARD JOHN CARNELL AND AMERICA'S
          EVANGELICAL TRADITION 1

   II   AUTHORITY AND ETHICS 31

          The Meaning of Authority
          The Meaning of Scripture
          The Use of Scripture in Ethics

  III   SELF-ACCEPTANCE AND MORAL KNOWLEDGE 65
          The Third Method of Knowing
          The Application of the Third
            Method of Knowing

   IV   RECTITUDE AND THE LAW OF LIFE 109

          The Law of Justice
          The Law of Consideration
          The Law of Love

    V   THEORY AND PRACTICE 147

CONCLUSION 163

BIBLIOGRAPHY 171

INTRODUCTION

This book is an investigation of the ethical thought of Edward John Carnell, former president and professor of ethics and philosophy of religion at Fuller Theological Seminary in Pasadena, California. In particular, it deals with Carnell as an ethicist in the evangelical tradition, examining his ideas on authority for ethics, ethical epistemology, fundamental moral norms, and normative issues.

My interest in Carnell was first sparked when I was taking a course on apologetic systems while attending seminary. The precision of Carnell's thought seemed to me to be of particular value when studying the arguments for affirming Christianity. Yet later I realized not that logic is irrelevant to belief, but rather, as Carnell had earlier observed, that it is inadequate. Reason can lead us to a knowledge of that which exists, but it cannot give us knowledge of where our moral commitments should lie, nor can it provide us with the passion necessary to make those commitments.

Evangelicalism currently realizes that its mission involves not only other-worldly concerns but this-worldly ones as well. The gospel implies personal faith, to be sure, but it also involves a life of holiness. That life is not lived in a state of moral perfection, but rather in a process of moral sanctification. The process requires direction. Yet for evangelicals today the direction, save for a firm commitment to the nebulous notion of the authority of Scripture, is lacking. Some evangelicals tend to withdraw from the social sphere of existence by affirming an ethic which is purely individual, and therefore only personal. Others focus their attention primarily upon social institutions, neglecting the individual social responsibility of discrete persons. The former position is viewed by the latter as a socially-irrelevant return to fundamentalism, and the latter is seen by the former to be a capitulation to liberalism. What is lacking within evangelicalism is concurrence regarding the emphasis which should be placed upon those issues which concern human life, yet which are not specifically and directly addressed in the New Testament. It is on these issues that direction is needed.

Carnell lived at a time when evangelicalism was

beginning to rediscover the fact that the message of personal salvation and the message of concern for physical need are not mutually exclusive, nor are they irreconcilable. Rather, they are both necessary elements of the gospel of Jesus Christ. In the nineteenth century, evangelicalism held both elements as parts of its message. During and after the controversy between the fundamentalists and the modernists, however, evangelicalism lost its concern for social issues, preferring to proclaim only the message of personal salvation. It was Carnell who, along with a few other evangelicals, marked a renaissance in evangelical awareness of the social side of reality and the need for evangelicals to recapture a complete gospel, including both elements, not just the element of personal salvation.

In the first chapter Carnell is not only located within his tradition, but is also seen as one who helped to shape the tradition by adding new elements to it. The second chapter addresses the issue of Carnell's authority for ethics. Although he claimed that Scripture alone was his authority, his ethical theory itself, as seen in chapter three, seems to support the idea that common moral experience legitimized the theory. In chapter four Carnell's development of the law of life, the fundamental moral norm, is presented. Love, for Carnell, was that norm which should guide all moral action. The influence of Soren Kierkegaard and Reinhold Niebuhr is especially apparent in this chapter. The fifth chapter examines the ways in which Carnell applied his theory to moral issues.

Carnell's life work was apologetics, that branch of Christian scholarship which seeks to offer defenses for the Christian faith. One of the approaches he took was to defend the faith through an examination and analysis of common moral experience. Throughout that examination he attempted to wed what he considered to be the true elements of Protestant orthodoxy with the true elements of theistic existentialism and Protestant neo-orthodoxy. The result was an ethic which he felt would be acceptable to and usable by anyone within the spectrum of Protestantism. It is regrettable that Carnell, rather than being embraced by liberals and conservatives, was rejected by both. The former disregarded him as a fundamentalist, and the latter rejected him for what they considered to be a denunciation of the faith.

I am convinced that what Carnell offered evangelicals over twenty-five years ago is more usable today than when it was first written. In the fifties the majority of evangelicals were not looking for ethical direction, for they were concentrating their energies on mass evangelism such as was being practiced by Billy Graham. Today, however, many evangelicals are realizing that if the gospel message is to be relevant to people living in the present world situation, it must contain an ethical element. What evangelicalism needs is direction in the ethical sphere. Carnell's ethical thought offers the needed direction, for it enables evangelicals to think in the field of ethics while maintaining their religious convictions. More than that, Carnell offers to evangelicals the existential element of ethics which is fundamental to the passion which must accompany ethical decision and action. As both an evangelical and a student of ethics I do not give wholehearted support to Carnell, but I can recommend him to those who want to learn about evangelicalism, as well as to those who want to learn about ethics.

I wish to express my appreciation to all who have helped to make this work possible. There are several, however, to whom I which to convey my special thanks. I am grateful to my wife, Ann, for her unceasing support, encouragement, and love; to my parents, Joseph and Frances, and to my brother, Jim, for their deep interest in my work; to Vernon Grounds and Gordon Lewis, without whose efforts this work would not have been published; to my friends, Bruce and Ina, who continue to demonstrate what it means to be neighbors; to John Orr for his helpful critique throughout this study; and to Mark and Marlene for their help in the preparation of the manuscript.

CHAPTER I

EDWARD JOHN CARNELL AND
AMERICA'S EVANGELICAL TRADITION

During the nineteenth century, evangelicals emphasized both ethical concern and personal salvation as necessary elements in a holy life. "This-worldly" concerns were more on their minds in this period than during any other period of their recent history. For example, Charles G. Finney, who can be considered as somehow representative of the dominant spirit of nineteenth-century evangelicalism, in his <u>Lectures on Revivals of Religion</u>, wrote that "revivals are hindered when ministers and churches take wrong ground in regard to any question involving human rights."(1) On the subject of slavery, he held that the church's role was to use church discipline against her members who engaged in such a social sin. He even went so far as to exclude slaveholders from the Lord's Supper.(2) Interestingly, such concern for social matters is not part of the image of Finney held by many later evangelicals, no doubt because they, desiring to accentuate the spiritual element of bygone revivals and revivalists, edited the social reform elements out of Finney's writings in later editions.(3)

This concern for social matters was not totally absent from the thinking of later evangelicals, however. Edward John Carnell was a prime example of an evangelical who realized that concern with the matters of this world was as much a part of Christian responsibility as was the task of sharing the message of eternal life through Jesus Christ.

> Every church member, whether or not he is ordained to preach the gospel, must associate with other human beings, and to the degree of this association he is part of a social order. Such membership carries responsibility.(4)

Although he has been identified primarily as an apologist, this ethical concern is found throughout his work and, to a large extent, gave direction to his apologetics.

Since this book is a study in Carnell's ethics,

the work of historians will be used only to create a picture of evangelicalism in the nineteenth and twentieth centuries against which we may place Carnell. This analysis should reveal the extent to which Carnell participated in the larger evangelical tradition, as well as the elements of his thinking which transcend this tradition.

Chief among the doctrines which were stressed by evangelicals between 1820 and 1860 was postmillennialism, the doctrine which made revivalism socially effective.(5) Earthly progress had to be encouraged since the second coming of Christ was near. To neglect to reform social evils was to delay Christ's coming. The doctrine basically envisioned a one-thousand year (either figurative or literal) golden age on earth, to be ushered in by human effort. It was to be a type of political, economic, social and religious utopia in which human society was reorganized according to divine law. The end of the age was to be crowned with the second advent of Christ. This expectation of Christ was the motivating factor behind those who worked for the millennium, for they saw their efforts in much the same way that John the Baptist saw his: preparing the way for the king.(6)

From the perspective of the early nineteenth century, history appeared to be confirming the postmillennial belief.(7) In 1851, for example, The Independent printed an article in which the editors held that "a grand feature of our time is that all is Progress."(8) Christianity and culture appeared to be united in their inevitable movement toward the everlasting Kingdom of God on earth.(9)

> It contemplates the organization and supremacy of goodness in human society--the doing of God's will on earth--the coming of His Kingdom hither, as well as our going hence to it.. . . Meanwhile it is ours, not only to fit ourselves and others for a better world, but to labor to make this world better.(10)

Feelings of nationalism influenced the doctrine, and church leaders began to claim that America was the physical location, or at least the physical starting point, of the millennium. For example, Gilbert Haven, a Methodist abolitionist, wrote, "America is the center of the world today."(11) He went on to assert that to save America was to save all lands. America was destined not only to triumph, but also to govern the whole earth, humbly, in the spirit of Christian love.(12)

In the face of America's triumph, all persons would be members of "an equal, universal, happy family, the family of Christ."(13) Some revivalists went so far as to anticipate the millennium in specific places and/or times. For example, Jonathan Blanchard, the founder of Wheaton College, said, "I came to Wheaton in 1860, still seeking 'a perfect state of society' and a college 'for Christ and his Kingdom.'"(14) He stayed at Wheaton for the rest of his life. As early as 1830, the revivalist H. B. Pierpoint wrote Charles Finney these words: "Oh what does the Lord mean New York shall do? Methinks the Millennium has already commenced and that this state is the starting point." Fifteen years later, Daniel Baker wrote his son, "Only think, the Emperor of China giving encouragement to the introduction of the Christian religion into his dominions! The Sandwich Islands affair upon a large scale. Surely, the millennium must be at hand."(15) Lyman Beecher even used the issue of the millennium as a tool to keep moral reform efforts alive. "If we endure a little longer," he wrote, "the resources of the millennial day will come to our aid. Many are the prophetic signs.. . . The last vial of the wrath of God is running."(16)

Millennial anticipation was by no means the only doctrinal influence upon evangelical ethical consciousness during this period. The concern for perfectionism and holiness was prominent in the minds of revivalists. "Perfectionism" was the teaching that moral perfection was not only an ideal, but that it was an attainable goal. In his <u>Memoirs</u>, Finney explained that "'Perfection' meant perfect trust and consecration, the experience of 'the fulness of the love of Christ,' not freedom from troublesome physical and mental appetites or from error and prejudice."(17) When pressed, then, the perfectionists often admitted that the goal included only a triumph over willful, known sin. The goal needed to be achieved before Christ could return, for a perfect king required a perfected society composed of perfected individuals.

The American holiness movement emphasized the instantaneous achievement of perfection, or entire sanctification, in a second emotional experience similar to that or conversion. For example, Horace Bushnell, in 1842, sought such perfection, motivated partly by the death of his infant son. One morning his wife found him on his knees, staring toward the sunrise, commenting, "I have seen the gospel."[18] Asa Mahan, president of the socially-radical Oberlin College, determined to achieve entire sanctification, following a daily religious discussion at the college during which he gave an affirmative answer to a student's question regarding the possibility of attaining such perfection. Having experienced what he considered to be that sanctification, his joyful preaching, along with that of other Oberlin perfectionists, sparked an era of spiritual vitality in the lives of scores of people.[19] This individualistic perfectionism was one kind of desired social involvement. Looking at the matter from the point of view of the requirements placed upon the Christian's life, Frederic Dan Huntington wrote in 1859 that there were no spiritual goals "unfolded in the gospel really and finally beyond the reach of sincere and consecrated persons."[20] The editors of <u>The Independent</u> wrote,

> There is such a thing as Christian perfection--perfection in the most absolute unqualified sense. This perfection is attainable, and should ever be our aim. We would urge our fellow Christians to it by all the motives of the Word of God.[21]

The alleged results of attaining perfection were permanence in the believer's experience and spiritual illumination of the intellect.[22] Perfectionism's spirit was capsulized in the hymn, Rock of Ages:

> Rock of Ages, cleft for me,
> Let me hide myself in Thee;
> Let the water and the blood;
> From Thy wounded side which flowed,
> Be of sin the <u>double cure</u>,
> Save from wrath and <u>make me pure</u>.[23]

Perfectionism was especially tied to millennial hope and visions of the Kingdom of God. William

Arthur, for example, believed that the Holy Spirit was regenerating the earth in preparation for Christ's personal reign, and Catherine Booth felt that the kingdom of God was no more than a generation away, provided that believers allowed the Holy Spirit to grasp complete control of their lives. Edward Beecher went so far as to assert that the kingdom could make no progress if there were not an increase in holiness. Far from being withdrawn from worldly matters, perfectionists held to the need for social action to achieve the millennium.(24) Rather than seeking ecstatic experiences, the one who was fully sanctified was to demonstrate that fact by being like Christ, a humble, suffering servant of his fellow man. Christ-likeness, they felt, would naturally spread perfectionism throughout the world, hastening the coming of the kingdom. The reform of society was to be the outstanding sign that believers, rather than Christ's adversaries, were concerned with their fellow human beings. Evil in the society and the kingdom could not go together. The perfection of individuals was not enough to usher in the millennium, for social sins, such as slavery, were viewed as violations of holiness. Only a holy world could host a holy Christ. Such a conviction was captured well in the Wesleyan hymnal, <u>Miriam's Timbrel</u>, which offered "<u>Sacred Songs</u>, <u>Suited</u> <u>to Revival Occasions</u>; <u>and</u> <u>Also</u> <u>for</u> <u>Antislavery</u>, <u>Peace</u>, <u>Temperance</u>, <u>and</u> <u>Reform</u> <u>Meetings</u>."(25) Perfectionist idealism, wedded with postmillennial optimism, was the catalyst for evangelical social reform.

There was one more element of theology which had considerable influence upon the social thinking of the revivalists of the nineteenth century. That element was popular Arminianism. Charles Finney and other Oberlinites viewed human sin as a relatively voluntary attitude of the mind. As such, it could be overcome by the power of the Holy Spirit, working in a moral and persuasive way, through the eloquent speaking of the preacher. The listener could, then, in a calculated manner, be brougnt to the point of conversion.(26)

Arminianism in American religious thought was epitomized in James W. Alexander's statement that "every man can be saved if he 'yields to the moving of the gracious Spirit, takes God at His word, and makes the universal offer his own particular salvation.'"(27) Calvinism's view of sin was altered to accommodate the revivalists. "The evangelists substituted an existential for the dogmatic concept of original sin, picturing it as a diseased condition of the soul rather than a legal burden of guilt for Adam's fall." This disease extended to the moral nature of man as well. Being a disease, sin could be healed by God who, as a shepherd seeking every lost sheep, extended his grace to every person. It was this grace alone which saved, but not without the exercising on the part of the individual, of the moral power of choice which that same grace had granted.(28)

It was certainly possible for Arminian theology to be sterile, but in the nineteenth century the pervasive revival spirit prevented such sterility from occurring. In fact, wherever there was belief in the working of God in the world and in the necessity of the free moral choice, there resulted a relatively liberal social ethic.(29) Postmillennialism dictated that through the efforts of Christians the kingdom would soon be ushered in, beginning in America; perfectionism established the requirement of complete dedication to God and freedom from all known, willful sin, on both an individual as well as a communal level, for the advancement of society toward the kingdom; and Arminianism, nurtured in revivalistic fervor, provided the motivation for dedicating oneself to work tirelessly toward the goal of ushering in the kingdom.

The post-Civil War years saw the development of a number of situations and issues that challenged the evangelical vision of a Christian America. Increased immigration brought scores of German Lutherans, Jews, and Roman Catholics, none of whom shared the utopian vision of the revivalists' Kingdom of God in America. Industrialization and urbanization introduced problems much too complex for the evangelical solution of social perfection. Biblical criticism, with the doubts it cast upon the traditional view of the origin and inspiration of Scripture, as well as Darwinism, with its challenge of the traditional view of human origin, played a part in the theological shift, leading many evangelicals to admit that the second coming of Christ was not going to be ushered in in the near future, at least not in the United States.(30) The increasing complexity of social problems required the revivalists to make choices between competing goods. For example, Oberlin theologians were committed both to peace and to abolition, but when the two conflicted at the point of the Civil War, the revivalists were at a loss.(31)

Soon the efforts to bring the Kingdom of God were rechanneled into efforts to convert as many as possible. For example, Dwight Moody, the great successor to Finney, poured his energy into a series of revivals, but his thological foundation was not that of postmillennialism. It was premillennialism. He saw no golden age of society on the horizon. For Moody, there was little hope for the salvation of the world or the ushering in of a millennium through human efforts.

> I look on this world as a wrecked vessel. God has given me a life-boat, and said to me, "Moody, save all you can." God will come in judgment and burn up this world, but the children of God don't belong to this world; they are in it, but not of it, like a ship in the water. The world is getting darker and darker; if you have any friends on this wreck unsaved you had better lose no time in getting them off.(32)

Visions of the world moving toward perfection, were given up.(33) Many supporters of Moody's premillennialism even thought that efforts to improve society would succeed only in putting off Christ's second coming to take the faithful few out of this world.(34) Nevertheless, the more pessimistic atmosphere did not destroy evangelicalism's social concern. Actually, after the Civil War, rising premillennial eschatology led some revivalists to adopt more moderate social views that their pre-Civil War counterparts. Moody, for example, approached the temperance issue just as he would any kind of personal sin. Describing his method, W. H. Daniels wrote,

> He comes before them with a Bible in his hand, and in the name of Jesus Christ invites drunkards to be saved by the very same grace, and in fulfillment of the very same promise which he offers to sinners seeking to be saved from other forms of sin.(35)

Yet, more extreme demonstrations of social concern were not eliminated by the war. <u>The Christian Herald</u>, in the 1890's, referred to war as a "relic of barbarism,"(36) and in 1915 called for an embargo on arms shipments.(37) In his biography of Catherine Booth, William T. Stead described Booth "as 'a Socialist, and something more'--one who was 'in complete revolt against the existing order.'"(38) Ballington Booth, leader of the American Salvation Army, concurred with his mother's views, saying, "To right the social wrong by charity is like bailing the ocean with a thimble.. . . We must readjust our social machinery so that the producers of wealth become also owners of wealth . . ."(39)

Still, the progressive social stance adopted by many evangelicals for the previous century was under attack, and ultimately the theological division among Protestants in the 1920's sent the evangelicals into a twenty-five-year withdrawal. Carl F. H. Henry, himself an evangelical social ethicist, characterized evangelicalism during these years as "the modern priest and Levite, by-passing suffering humanity." Expanding on the thought, he continued:

> . . . [T]he challenge of modern Fundamentalism to the present world mind is almost non-existent on the great social issues.. . . For Fundamentalism in the main fails to make relevant to the great moral problems in twentieth-century global living the implications of its redemptive message.(40)

Henry attempted to change that situation when, in 1947, he published his book, The Uneasy Conscience of Modern Fundamentalism, in which he tried both to awaken evangelicals to their social responsibility and to outline an evangelical theory of social involvement. In reality this move was a return to the nineteenth century stance on social matters, for it was an attempt to revive the once-dominant position which held that Jesus is to be Lord not only of the individual, in a personal and spiritual sense, but also of society, in a collective and physical sense. The lordship of Christ was to predominate in all aspects of human experience. In this effort to return to a healthy evangelicalism, Henry called for a restudy of that doctrine which had colored the evangelical social stance of the previous century: eschatology.(41) He devoted an entire chapter to the problem of apprehension over kingdom preaching, a situation which had developed within Fundamentalism in which preachers were reluctant to speak about a present kingdom because it could too easily be misinterpreted as the liberal social gospel. Arguing chiefly from the examples of Jesus and the apostles, with the explicit statement that the concept of the kingdom was what colored Christ's actions, he wrote,

> Yet no subject was more frequently on the lips of Jesus than the kingdom. He proclaimed kingdom truth with a constant, exuberant joy. It appears as the central theme of His preaching. To delete His Kingdom references, parabolic and nonparabolic, would be to excise most of His words. The concept "kingdom of God" or "kingdom of heaven" is heard repeatedly from His lips, and it colors all of His works.. . . The apostolic view of the kingdom should likewise be definitive for contemporary evangelicalism. There does not seem much apostolic apprehension over kingdom preaching.(42)

Henry's view was the predominant one among evangelicals at the time Carnell was developing his thinking in ethics. That view held that Christianity opposes every kind of evil, personal and social, and advocated, as the only sufficient formula for the resolution of that evil, the regenerative work of the Holy Spirit. The gospel is to be preached "in such a way that divine redemption can be recognized as the best solution of our problems, individual and social."(43) In Henry's follow-up work of 1964 he reiterated the same position, writing that "Christian social action condones no social solutions in which personal acceptance of Jesus Christ as Saviour and Lord is an optional consideration."(44) To Henry, any such effort was a needlessly wasted one.(45)

About the same time, evangelist Billy Graham was advocating the same position.(46) This effort to renew the entire person, and eventually the society composed of such persons, by the regenerating work of the Holy Spirit, Graham argued, sees its practical outworking through moderate social action. The effort is by no means passive; withdrawal from the social sphere is condemned.(47)

Yet admittedly, the social change that Graham advocated appears to be somewhat timid. For example, he argued, the devout person obeys the law of the State as a spiritual duty, even to the extent of obeying speed limits and parking regulations. Above all, the Christian's chief duty as a citizen is that of civil obedience.(48) The only acceptable means of protest is through the democratic parliamentary right of minor action, particularly in developing statements of protest.(49)

Carl Henry's work marked the start of a renaissance of scholarship within orthodox protestant circles in the United States. Another one of the leaders of this renewal movement was Edward John Carnell.(50) Born in Antigo, Wisconsin, on June 28, 1919,(51) Carnell had deep fundamentalist roots.(52) He was reared in a Baptist parsonage, and in 1944 was himself ordained a Baptist minister.(53)

Carnell's thinking and writing were influenced by a number of people under whom he studied. At Wheaton College (A.B., 1941) he learned from Christian rationalist Gordon H. Clark the test of noncontradiction. Under apologist Cornelius Van Til at Westminster Theological Seminary (B.D. and Th.M., 1944) he found his starting point to be the triune God of the Bible. While earning his Ph.D. (1949) under Edgar S. Brightman at Boston University, Carnell learned to include fitness to empirical fact in his world view. During his research in Soren Kierkegaard and Reinhold Niebuhr at Harvard Univeristy (S.T.M., 1946; Th.D., 1948), he realized that relevance to personal and social experience was important.(54)

From 1945 to 1947, while attending Harvard University, Carnell pastored the Baptist Church of Marblehead, Mass.(55) While earning a living working at a Boston mail terminal Carnell was offered a summer teaching position in philosophy by Dr. Burton Goddard, dean of Gordon College. He proved himself so competent that by the end of the summer he was asked to accept a permanent teaching assignment.(56) While continuing his teaching at Gordon and his studies at Boston University, he published his first book, <u>An Introduction to Christian Apologetics</u>. In 1948, the book was awarded the 5,000-dollar Eerdmans Evangelical Book Award.

After three years of teaching philosophy at Gordon College and Gordon Divinity School, Carnell joined the faculty of Fuller Theological Seminary as professor of apologetics and systematic theology.(57) Students testified that in the classroom Carnell made them deal with issues that were of "the very stuff of life." Demonstrating in his own life some of the convictions which he would later defend in his writing, he apparently had "an instinct for the visceral issues of theology and Christian living."(58)

From 1954 to 1959 Carnell served as president of Fuller Theological Seminary.(59) At the outset of his presidency some faculty and student body members feared that Carnell's image of aloofness would ruin his effectiveness.(60) The image was a false one, though, being merely the outward expression of Carnell's inward struggle with those realities which give life meaning. At this point Carnell was his own worst enemy, never being satisfied with either the adequacy of traditional orthodox protestant arguments or with the current development of his own thought. He proved to be up to the presidential task, however, being largely responsible for the seminary's gaining accreditation,(61) as well as for establishing many of the directions the school currently takes.(62) As president, Carnell had two goals: to make the seminary a school which would produce clergy who would make Protestant orthodoxy a power force, and, through his own writing, to defend rationally that same Protestant orthodoxy.(63)

Throughout his life, Carnell increasingly accentuated the difference between fundamentalism and orthodoxy. In his first book Carnell made no distinction between fundamentalism and orthodoxy,(64) but in his second major work in apologetics he dropped the term "fundamentalist" altogether.(65) He became increasingly disturbed by the separatistic attitude displayed by many fundamentalists. The schisms within the church that such an attitude produced led Carnell to dissociate himself increasingly from fundamentalism. In the chapter entitled "Perils" in his book, <u>The Case for Orthodox Theology</u>, Carnell defined fundamentalism as "orthodoxy gone cultic."(66) He went on to seal his break with fundamentalism by writing a clear denouncement of both fundamentalism and fundamentalism's great spokes-person, J. Gresham

11

Machen. This attack extended even to the area of social concern. Making the point that fundamentalists were not concerned about social justice, he wrote, "The fundamentalist is not disturbed by this, of course, for he is busy painting 'Jesus Saves' on rocks in a public park."(67) Having rejected the title "fundamentalist," Carnell adopted the term "orthodox" to describe his position within conservative Protestant theology. Throughout the rest of his career he made Scriptural authority the norm for orthodoxy.(68) As could be expected, many fundamentalists turned on Carnell, charging that he had abandoned the proper view of Scripture. To the end, though, he called himself orthodox precisely because he held to the traditional views on the great doctrines of the faith, including the doctrine of Scripture.(69)

Ironically, the editorial staff of The Christian Century "cherished the fact that it had in Dr. Carnell a two-way bridge between itself and one of the more conservative wings of evangelical Christianity."(70) At his death not only did the journal's staff express regret at having lost a contributor on the academic level, but it also offered genuine sympathy to Carnell's family, friends and Fuller Seminary.(71)

In all of his major works, Carnell attempted to "build on some useful point of contact between the gospel and culture."(72) With this in mind, he leaned heavily upon the law of contradiction in his first book, An Introduction to Christian Apologetics.(73) His attempt was to present orthodox Protestantism in terms of a rationalistic world view. To Carnell, the appeal to feeling or paradox was an insufficient reason for faith. The only reason for believing in the Christian world view, he argued, is that it is internally self-consistent and fits the facts of experience better than any other world view. This apologetic conviction was so strong that he attacked "every effort to shield religion from the responsibility of defending itself."(74)

In A Philosophy of the Christian Religion (1952), Carnell shifted emphasis from logic to axiology, the science of values. Seeking to make contact with culture in a second way, he attempted to show that orthodox Protestantism is important and desirable, not just true.(75) Showing appreciation for Kierkegaard, Carnell considered the personal needs of the individual.(76) Yet reason remained as the test for truth: "The heart knows a depth of insight which, <u>while it may never be separated from rational consistency</u>, is yet not univocally identified with such consistency."(77)

Carnell's third major work, <u>Christian Commitment: An Apologetic</u> (1957), and the one which he considered to be his best book,(78) appealed to the third method of knowing, as well as to the judicial sentiment. The former is the method which puts the individual in contact with knowledge in the moral realm, and is known as knowledge by moral self-acceptance. It is to be seen in relation to the other two ways of knowing, knowledge by acquaintance and knowledge by inference. The latter is that human moral faculty which is offended when the individual is the victim of injustice. Carnell's indebtedness to Kierkegaard is clearly evident in this work, as emphasis was placed upon the moral environment in which the individual lives and which must be understood if one is to find meaning in the area of ethics.

In his final attempt to bridge the gap between the gospel and culture, Carnell took a psychological approach, appealing to the law of love. <u>The Kingdom of Love and the Pride of Life</u> (1960) built upon the premise that the convictions of the heart such as natural beliefs concerning right and wrong, truth and falsehood and love and hate, are closer to reality than the knowledge gained through intellectual pursuits. The innocent love of a happy child was held up as an ideal, and the love of Jesus demonstrated to Mary and Martha at the death of Lazarus (John, chap. 11) served as an example. Intellectual detachment was challenged with the argument that only child-like trust in God can provide the solution to life's mysteries.

Carnell's concern for society and the forces which give it shape and direction was evident in his <u>Television--Servant or Master?</u> (1950). Carnell referred to this work as "an anticipatory balance sheet"(79) in which he attempted to sum up the major virtues and vices of television. Realizing that the book was theoretical, Carnell sought to appraise the good and bad effects which television may have, not those which it will have.

Both of Carnell's dissertations became bases of

books. His Th.D. dissertation, The Concept of Dialectic in the Theology of Reinhold Niebuhr, was seen in published form as The Theology of Reinhold Niebuhr (1950), and dealt with one controlling concept: the dialectical relation between time and eternity. Carnell's Ph.D. dissertation, The Problem of Verification in Soren Kierkegaard, later became the book, The Burden of Soren Kierkegaard (1965). The author, attempting to allow Kierkegaard to speak for himself, discussed two main theses: "existential living" and "truth is subjectivity."

At the request of Westminster Press, Carnell wrote The Case for Orthodox Theology (1959). This book, along with two others (The Case for Theology in a Liberal Perspective, by L. Harold De Wolf, and The Case for a New Reformation Theology, by William Hordern) was written to provide theology students with a clear statement of contemporary theological viewpoints by convinced adherents.(80)

Carnell was asked to contribute chapters to several books. Among these were the article on "fundamentalism" in A Handbook of Christian Theology (ed. Marvin Halverson and Arthur A. Cohen),(81) "Reinhold Niebuhr's View of Scripture" in Inspiration and Interpretation (ed. John W. Walvoord), and "Niebuhr's Criteria of Verification" in Reinhold Niebuhr: His Religious, Social, and Political Thought (ed. Charles W. Kegley and Robert W. Bretall).(82)

Carnell was a member of the American Philosophical Association and the American Academy of Religion,(83) and was included in a panel of theologians that questioned Karl Barth during his lectures entitled "An Introduction to Evangelical Theology," given at the University of Chicago Divinity School. It was this lectureship which prompted Carnell to write "Barth as Inconsistent Evangelical," in which he criticized Barth for overusing the language of paradox and for espousing mere "feeling theology."(84)

As might be expected, the doctrines which had been influential in the history of evangelical social concern also had their place in Carnell's ethical thinking. For Carnell, theology's subject was the gospel. Its purpose was to define and apply the gospel. The particular theological tradition which he felt reflected the theology of the prophets and apostles was that of orthodox Protestantism, and the most consistent expression or orthodoxy was the Reformed faith. Yet he did assert that the Reformed tradition had its shortcomings,(85) and thus it legitimately may be expected that he would depart from that tradition at points.

Carnell took a moderate stand on eschatology, being neither overly pessimistic nor overly optimistic. "Nothing will be gained by either wringing our hands in despair or by dreaming of utopian visions."(86) Pretribulationism, a form of premillennialism, he saw as a case of pessimistic over-emphasis, noting that the church's hope is in the return of Christ, not in deliverance from tribulation.(87) Neo-orthodoxy also impressed him as having made the pessimistic error, placing too much stress on inevitable sin and judgment.(88) On the other end of the spectrum, Carnell attacked the Anabaptists, holding that their collective cultic mind corrupted the cryptic elements of the Synoptic Gospels into a doctrine of a literal earthly kingdom.(89) The optimism of liberalism apparently led it into the same arror.(90)

In attempting to determine the details of Carnell's own eschatology, one searches his writings in vain. Nowhere did he offer a systematic treatment of his view of the last things, although he did give a few hints which serve to confirm the place of eschatology in his ethical thinking. In attempting to show that Christian living must include efforts at furthering social justice, for example, he denied that those efforts would achieve a utopian society. "The regeneration of the social order . . . awaits the blessed return of our Lord and Saviour Jesus Christ."(91) His optimism regarding a better social order, consequently, was tempered by the belief that it would be Christ's return, not human efforts, that would bring the improved order. At one point, in attacking dispensationalism, Carnell asserted that theological novelty is avoided by holding to the classical creeds of the church.(92) In so doing he placed himself within the amillennial tradition, and at one point even hinted that this was his position.(93) This conviction, as well as his general lack of writing on eschatology, leads to two simple conclusions: (1) Carnell does not fall into the evangelical social tradition of placing great emphasis upon the millennium, and (2) eschatology was not one of the prime bases for Carnell's ethical concern.

The conviction that a literal millennium would not be forthcoming reveals a basic element of Carnell's ethical thinking: until after Christ's second coming, one whose purpose is judgment, actual perfection is not possible. This notion can be seen not only in Carnell's view on society, but also in his thinking regarding individuals. As was the case with eschatology, he took a mediating position between optimism and pessimism, stating that "we strive for sinless perfection, though we shall never reach it."(94) The individual is a somewhat passive participant in the achievement of good, for God responds to human humility with the gift of virtue.(95) In arguing against the Roman Catholic concept of perfection he actually set himself against his pre-Civil-War forefathers' idea that the individual could achieve complete freedom from all known sin.

> A good will is not perfection. We are perfect only when we mediate the law of love with infinite exactness in our daily lives. We are holy in fact only when we live according to the same law to which we give assent in our will.(96)

Yet, he went on to assert, "in no act do we ever resist sinfulness with perfection. There is always an element of pride in the will.. . . it is sin."(97) At this point Carnell began to show the influence of Reinhold Niebuhr's view of sin as pride and the inevitability of sin on his own thinking regarding human nature.(98) For Carnell, perfectionists made three theological errors: (1) they had a wrong view of law. Assuming that law meant the commandments, they neglected the law's primary requirement, pure love of God and neighbor. (2) They had a wrong view of sin. Carnell realized that conscious sins were merely the outworking of inner sin; perfectionists did not. (3) They had a wrong view of sanctification. Perfectionists felt that acts of faith made them perfect, but Carnell objected, holding that sanctification comes when the individual cooperates with God's gracious working in his life.(99) Relating the doctrine of perfection to social concern, he wrote,

> Christ promises forgiveness of sins, not a new endowment for socal philosophers..

> . . When "perfection in Christ" converts
> to "perfection in self," those who
> repent will either magnify what they
> receive or be disappointed in what they
> find.(100)

The pre-Civil-War social optimists had done the former; the post-Civil-War pessimists had done the latter.

Carnell's negative view of perfection was a result of his prior affirmation of the reality of original sin. Taking the Reformed viewpoint, he held to the federal headship of Adam, who "brought sin and death upon the human race by violating his covenantal probation." The result can be seen in children even from birth; their dominant orientation is toward self-centeredness.(101) All individuals commit sin because they are, by nature, sinners. The will is merely an accomplice in sin.(102) Original sin does not extend only to individuals, though; nature itself is federally involved in Adam's sin,(103) and thus it has a natural tendency toward evil. Social problems are not only created by human action; they are created by original sin. The entire human enterprise, no matter how virtuous, is tainted by pride and the will to power.(104) The greater the effort to live for others, the more obvious become the sins of pride and power.(105) Thus even though Carnell was not Niebuhrian in his doctrine of original sin, Niebuhr's influence can be seen in Carnell's ideas regarding the social results of original sin.(106)

In treating Calvinism, Carnell, consistent with his other doctrinal views, took a mediating position. Asserting that the individual is passive in his spiritual birth, he accused the Arminian of mistakenly holding that God's saving grace can be resisted. At the same time he charged the Calvinist with fallaciously supposing that repentance cannot come until after regeneration by the Holy Spirit.(107) Taken to an extreme, Calvinism is nonsense, disregarding man's inherent moral sense.(108) Its basic problem is that it grew into a theological system, drawing necessary conclusions which Scripture itself did not require.(109) Carnell saw God as one who invites all, yet leaves the individual free to choose.(110) Basic to Carnell's theory of history is divine sovereignty, the metaphysical foundation of his world view. "At no place is sovereignty compromised."(111) That being the case, there is no objective standard of good which is binding upon God. "The Christian says that the will of God is the final standard of good and that what God wills is good because he wills it."(112) In this point he set himself against Platonic philosophy, which holds that the good is an order of existence separate from God and man. He even went so far as to assert that it is logical to suppose that God can do whatever he pleases, without being held accountable. Logic, therefore, is not a valid objection to sovereignty.(113) Carnell showed some inconsistency here, for his charge that extreme Calvinism is nonsense was based upon the fact that it disregarded logic.(114) Yet he used the same argument in defending his own position.

The way Carnell harmonized the extremes into his own mediating position was to hold that God uses man's freedom to bring about divine ends. Man is free when he makes his own choices, for not even God can choose for him. Freedom is not capriciousness, for God, being omniscient, knows in advance all free human choices.(115) Man is not so free as to escape God's foreknowledge and judgment, and thus in every human act man is responsible before the divine judge.(116)

What Carnell had done was to assume a doctrinal position which required that social change be the result of human effort. If people do not freely act to improve society, God is not responsible. The responsibility is fully human. God's sovereignty will not accomplish the regeneration of the social order without the means of human effort, for the Holy Spirit will not force regeneration upon a person. The individual must freely respond to the Spirit's leading. In this respect Carnell was like the pre-Civil-War revivalists even more than Henry, emphasizing the element of human will. Yet he stopped short of their position by retreating into God's sovereignty. God will accomplish his plan for society. If he wills that there not be a millennium (in keeping with Carnell's eschatology), then no amount of human effort will accomplish one. Human hope is to be in the return of Christ, not in the possibility of utopia. Carnell is in the evangelical tradition of having a future-oriented element to his social concern, but unlike the nineteenth century pre-Civil-War evangelicals or Henry, he did not emphasize the millennium or the kingdom on earth, but rather Christ's return. At this point he is like the post-Civil-War evangelicals. His uniqueness, though, is in his synthetic position.

The attempt to place Carnell within the evangelical spectrum of social involvement is met with some difficulty, for in his writing he emphasized the will and affections much more than the form of action. He substantiated this emphasis by an appeal to the Apostle Paul's writing in 1 Cor. 13:3, "If I give away all I have, and if I deliver my body to be burned, but have not love, I gain nothing" (RSV).(117) Yet his sympathies regarding the form of social action are discernible. Sounding like Henry or Graham, Carnell wrote, "[A] truly workable social ethic is structured on the disclosures and graces of the gospel itself."(118) He was not as reserved in his definition of salvation or in his ideas on justice, however. Henry held that to work for the personal salvation of individuals was the proper way eventually to form a just society. Carnell, in contrast, asserted that Christ's lordship is the very thing that gives Christians the proper motivation to work for justice.(119) He did not assume that salvation brought with it a tendency toward a more just society. In fact, he indicted Billy Graham for confusing forensic justification and inherent moral superiority.(120) Basic to any social action, according to Carnell, is love of Christ. Concern for justice is a sign that that love is at work in the believer.(121) That love is expressed by acting out the golden rule. Christians should do as they would prefer to be treated by others, for "the law of love negates any static subordination of life to life. Human equality is the limiting concept of all Christian social action."(122) Drawing on the thought of Soren Kierkegaard, Carnell felt that too many ethicists were overly-concerned with legalism, since "love is the fulfillment of the law, and . . . the ethical self falls short of its duties until it performs works of love."(123) It was that love motivation which led Carnell to go beyond calling a social problem such as drunkenness, with its associated poverty, a sin that is curable by personal salvation, and to assert that it is a disease which should be treated by every medical and psychotherapeutic means possible.(124)

The influence of Reinhold Niebuhr can be seen in Carnell's view of the Christian and government. Love is not a factor when dealing with the government, for justice, not love, is the government's concern. Wicked people cannot be stopped by love. Only force, the means used by an impersonal body, can effect justice. The Christian, then, as an agent of his government, is to treat others with justice. If this means dropping a bomb which kills 100,000 people, then so be it. Maintaining a just society is the Christian's goal when he discharges his duty to God as a good citizen. Warfare is thus legitimate, but only if it is defensive. Aggressive or preventive warfare is not an option for the Christian, even if instructed to participate in such warfare by his or her government.(125) Carnell thus expressed his personal aversion to the extreme method of violence, and may even have been inconsistent when he more than once quoted an Old Testament verse that places violence in opposition to justice.(126) Revolution as a means for social change was not an option for Carnell. He saw revolutionaries as people ignorant of the moral limits both of their individual lives and of history. The utopian vision errs when it sees things in black and white, and imagines that injustice and tyranny can be challenged with ease.(127) Social evils must be attacked, but the attack must be carried out in the same way that the apostles attacked Caesar--with grace and dignity. To avoid revolution, a subtle course against the social order must be chosen. Revolution only serves to obscure the promised blessings, at best, and to reduce the gospel to an ideology.(128)

It is clear that Carnell, having reflected on the side effects of extreme forms of social change, rejected them. He also realized that mere spiritual salvation of individuals is an ineffective means to deal with social evils. Justice has to be pursued, and it is the Christian's responsibility to pursue it. It will not just happen. Thus Carnell was somewhat of a social progressive, seeking to effect justice in his world, and to demonstrate the love of Christ for his creation.

It is no secret that Carnell suffered from emotional problems. During his school years he struggled to work out his inner conflicts, and throughout his life he suffered prolonged insomnia and nervous disorders.(129) Perhaps it was because of these problems that he was forced to resign the presidency of Fuller Seminary, devoting the rest of his life to teaching and writing. He died suddenly, on April 25, 1967, while in Oakland, preparing to speak at a conference.

Carnell was a rare person--a scholar who claimed to be an orthodox protestant, yet an individual who, in his eager debate with non-conservatives, displayed none of the aloofness, separatism, and bitterness of many fundamentalists.(130) This unique combination of academic and personal characteristics made him an individual who offered a fresh, viable option for social ethics--one which current evangelicals should consider.

FOOTNOTES

(1) Charles G. Finney, <u>Lectures on Revivals of Religion</u>, as quoted by Donald W. Dayton, <u>Discovering an Evangelical Heritage</u>, (New York: Harper & Row, 1976), p. 18.

(2) Ibid., p. 19.

(3) Ibid.

(4) Edward John Carnell, "A Christian Social Ethics," <u>The Christian Century</u>, August 7, 1963, p. 979.

(5) I am aware that this assertion is debatable, and that not all evangelicals were postmillennialists. A case could be made for stating the opposite. The Baptist preacher William Miller, for example, concluded after years of study that Christ would return in 1843. In 1836 he published <u>Evidence from Scripture and History of the Second Coming of Christ, About the Year 1843</u>, a book which won many people to his premillennial view. I would contend, however, that such thinking had little effect upon the dominant postmillennial position, along with its accompanying social implications. After Christ failed to return in 1843, premillennialism was largely rejected until just before the Civil War. See Earl E. Cairns, "Miller, William," <u>The New International Dictionary of the Christian Church</u>, ed. J. D. Douglas (Grand Rapids: Zondervan, 1974), p. 660, and Timothy L. Smith, <u>Revivalism and Social Reform</u> (Baltimore: Johns Hopkins Univ. Press, 1980), pp. 29, 228-229, 236.

(6) Smith, pp. 15, 151, 225, 236.

(7) Charles C. Cole, Jr., <u>The Social Ideas of the Northern Evangelists, 1826-1860</u> (New York: Columbia Univ. Press, 1954), p. 232.

(8) "The Coming Age," <u>The Independent</u>, Jan. 16, 1851, as quoted by Smith, p. 226.

(9) Smith, p. 226.

(10) <u>The Watchman and Reflector</u>, March 26, 1857, as quoted by Smith, pp. 152-153.

(11) Gilbert Haven, <u>National Sermons</u>, as quoted by

Smith, p. 221.

(12) Smith, p. 222.

(13) Gilbert Haven, *National Sermons*, as quoted by Smith, p. 222.

(14) As quoted by Dayton, p. 12.

(15) As quoted by Cole, p. 233.

(16) Ibid.

(17) Smith, p. 104.

(18) Ibid., p. 106.

(19) Ibid., p. 104.

(20) Frederic Dan Huntington, *Christian Believing and Living* (Boston: n.p., 1859), p. 424, as quoted by Smith, p. 107.

(21) "The Scriptural View of Perfection," *The Independent*, Jan. 11, 1849, as quoted by Smith, p. 111.

(22) Smith., p. 110.

(23) As quoted by Smith, p. 113.

(24) Smith, pp. 157-159, 232.

(25) Ibid., pp. 155, 158, 161, 206, 212.

(26) Cole, pp. 63-64.

(27) As quoted by Smith, p. 90.

(28) Smith, pp. 28, 91, 102.

(29) Ibid., p. 92.

(30) Dayton, p. 125.

(31) Ibid., p. 124.

(32) W. H. Daniels, ed., *Moody: His Words, Works and Workers* (New York: Nelson & Phillips, 1877), pp. 475-476.

(33) David O. Moberg, *The Great Reversal* (revised ed.), (Philadelphia: A. J. Holman Co., 1977), p. 32.

(34) Dayton, p. 126.

(35) Daniels, p. 515.

(36) As quoted by Norris Magnuson, *Salvation in the Slums: Evangelical Social Work, 1865-1920* (Metuchen: The Scarecrow Press, 1977), p. 154.

(37) "Are We Keeping Up the War?," *Christian Herald*, Jan. 20, 1915, p. 54, as cited by Magnuson, p. 165.

(38) William T. Stead, *Life of Mrs. Booth* (New York: n.p., 1900), p. 195, as quoted by Magnuson, p. 165.

(39) As quoted by Magnuson, pp. 165-166.

(40) Carl F. H. Henry, *The Uneasy Conscience of Modern Fundamentalism* (Grand Rapids: Eerdmans, 1947), pp. 17, 38.

(41) Ibid., p. 51.

(42) Ibid., pp. 52, 55.

(43) Ibid., pp. 45, 88.

(44) Carl F. H. Henry, *Aspects of Christian Social Ethics* (Grand Rapids: Eerdmans, 1964), p. 25.

(45) Henry, *The Uneasy Conscience of Modern Fundamentalism*, p. 27.

(46) Billy Graham, *World Aflame* (Garden City: Doubleday & Co., 1965), pp. 177-178.

(47) Henry, *Aspects of Christian Social Ethics*, p. 16.

(48) Ibid., pp. 79, 80, 101.

(49) Henry, *The Uneasy Conscience of Modern Fundamentalism*, pp. 78-80.

(50)William E. Hordern, *A Layman's Guide to Protestant Theology* (Revised ed., New York: Macmillan, 1973), p. 55.

(51)John A. Sims, *Edward John Carnell: Defender of the Faith* (Washington: University Press of America, Inc., 1979), p. 3.

(52)William S. Sailer, "The Role of Reason in the Theologies of Nels Ferre and Edward J. Carnell" (unpublished S.T.D. dissertation, Temple University, 1964), p. 14.

(53)Joe E. Barnhart, "The Religious Epistemology and Theodicy of Edward John Carnell and Edgar Sheffield Brightman: A Study in Contrasts" (unpublished Ph.D. dissertation, Boston University, 1964), p. 6.

(54)Gordon R. Lewis, *Testing Christianity's Truth Claims* (Chicago: Moody Press, 1977), p. 176.

(55)Sims, p. 7.

(56)Paul K. Jewett, "An Appreciation Given at Dr. Carnell's Funeral on April 28, 1967." *The Opinion*, VI, No. 7 (May 1967), p. 17.

(57)Barnhart, p. 6.

(58)*Theology News & Notes* (Pasadena: Fuller Theological Seminary, Bol. 13, No. 2), pp. 3, 4.

(59)Barnhart, p. 6.

(60)Aubrey B. Haines, "Edward John Carnell: An Evaluation," *The Christian Century*, June 7, 1967, p. 751.

(61)*Theology News & Notes* (Pasadena: Fuller Theological Seminary, Vol 5, No. 2), p. 2.

(62)Haines, p. 751.

(63)Ibid.

(64)Edward John Carnell, *An Introduction to Christian Apologetics* (Grand Rapids: Eerdmans, 1948), p. 11.

(65) Sailer, p. 15.

(66) Edward John Carnell, The Case for Orthodox Theology (Philadelphia: The Westminster Press, 1959), p. 113.

(67) Ibid., pp. 113ff, 123.

(68) Sims, p. 1.

(69) Ibid., p. 147.

(70) "Edward John Carnell Dies in California," The Christian Century, May 10, 1967, p. 612.

(71) Ibid.

(72) Edward John Carnell, The Kingdom of Love and the Pride of Life (Grand Rapids: Eerdmans, 1960), p. 6.

(73) Ibid.

(74) Hordern, p. 66.

(75) Lewis, p. 210.

(76) Edward John Carnell, A Philosophy of the Christian Religion (Grand Rapids: Eerdmans, 1960), pp. 455ff.

(77) Ibid., p. 39.

(78) Ronald H. Nash, ed., The Case for Biblical Christianity (Grand Rapids: Eerdmans, 1969), p. 6.

(79) Edward John Carnell, Television--Servant or Master? (Grand Rapids: Eerdmans, 1950), p. 6.

(80) Sims, p. 7.

(81) Sailer, p. 4.

(82) Barnhart, p. 7.

(83) Hordern, p. 55.

(84) Edward John Carnell, "Barth as Inconsistent Evangelical," The Christian Century, June 6, 1962, p.

713.

(85)Carnell, The Case for Orthodox Theology, pp. 13, 78, 127.

(86)Carnell, The Kingdom of Love and the Pride of Life, p. 117.

(87)Carnell, The Case for Orthodox Theology, pp. 63-64

(88)Edward John Carnell, "Why Neo-Orthodoxy?," The Watchman Examiner, Feb. 19, 1948, p. 180.

(89)Carnell, The Case for Orthodox Theology, p. 57.

(90)Carnell, "Why Neo-Orthodoxy?," p. 181.

(91)Carnell, "A Christian Social Ethics," p. 980.

(92)Carnell, The Case for Orthodox Theology, p. 117.

(93)On page 126 of The Case for Orthodox Theology Carnell cited as collateral reading in "The classical creeds and the details of eschatology," J. A. Brown, "The Second Advent and the Creeds of Christendom," Bibliotheca Sacra, Vol. XXIV (1867), pp. 629-651. The main point of this article is that the creeds, ancient and modern, Protestant, Catholic, and Greek, teach a view of eschatology that is totally irreconcilable with millenarian thinking. Being thus opposed to the confessions of Christendom, it should have no place in modern Christian thought. Christ's second coming will be to judge, not to bring a millennial reign.

(94)Edward John Carnell, "The Nature of the Unity We Seek," Nash, p. 23.

(95)Edward John Carnell, Christian Commitment: An Apologetic (New York: Macmillan, 1957), p. 199.

(96)Carnell, A Philosophy of the Christian Religion, p. 419.

(97)Ibid., p. 428.

(98)See Reinhold Niebuhr, The Nature and Destiny

of Man, Vol. I, Human Nature (New York: Charles Scribner's Sons, 1964), pp. 186-219, 251-254, for a discussion of the pride and inevitability of sin.

(99)Carnell, The Case for Orthodox Theology, p. 74.

(100)Nash, p. 88.

(101)Carnell, The Case for Orthodox Theology, p. 72.

(102)Carnell, A Philosophy of the Christian Religion, p. 260.

(103)Carnell, Christian Commitment: An Apologetic, p. 146.

(104)Carnell, "The Nature of the Unity We Seek," p. 23.

(105)Carnell, A Philosophy of the Christian Religion, p. 260.

(106)See Reinhold Niebuhr, Moral Man and Immoral Society (New York: Charles Scribner's Sons, 1960), pp. xi-xxv, 1-22, for Niebuhr's view on power and the inability of humans to transcend their own interests.

(107)Carnell, Christian Commitment: An Apologetic, p. 265.

(108)Edward John Carnell, "Bowing to Authority," rev. of Cornelius Van Til, The Case for Calvinism (Baker), The Christian Century, Mar. 10, 1965, p. 304.

(109)Carnell, The Kingdom of Love and the Pride of Life, p. 113.

(110)Carnell, Christian Commitment: An Apologetic, p. 303.

(111)Ibid., p. 270.

(112)Carnell, A Philosophy of the Christian Religion, pp. 312-313.

(113)Carnell, An Introduction to Christian Apologetics, p. 304.

(114) Carnell, "Bowing to Authority,", p. 304.

(115) Edward John Carnell, "How Every Christian Can Defend His Faith," part III, Moody Monthly, Mar. 1950, p. 461.

(116) Carnell, An Introduction to Christian Apologetics, p. 314n.

(117) Carnell, Christian Commitment: An Apologetic, p. 300.

(118) Carnell, "A Christian Social Ethics," p. 980.

(119) Ibid.

(120) Edward John Carnell, "A Proposal to Reinhold Niebuhr," The Christian Century, Oct. 17, 1956.

(121) Carnell, "A Christian Social Ethics," p. 980.

(122) Carnell, The Case for Orthodox Theology, p. 56.

(123) Edward John Carnell, The Burden of Soren Kierkegaard (Grand Rapids: Eerdmans, 1965), p. 167.

(124) Edward John Carnell, "Is Drunkenness a Sin?," United Evangelical Action, Mar. 1, 1948, p. 8.

(125) Edward John Carnell, "Should a Christian Go to War?," His, April 1951, pp. 7-8.

(126) The verse is Ezek. 45:9. Carnell quoted it in Christian Commitment: An Apologetic, p. 138, and in "A Christian Social Ethics," p. 979.

(127) Carnell, Christian Commitment: An Apologetic, p. 196.

(128) Carnell, The Case for Orthodox Theology, p. 62.

(129) Sims, pp. 3, 148.

(130) Nash, p. 5.

CHAPTER II

AUTHORITY AND ETHICS

A continuing issue in the study of ethics is the question of authority. There is anything but agreement among ethicists on such topics as the relationship between theology and ethics, the use of authority in ethics, the meaning and nature of authority for ethics, and the use of authoritative texts in ethics. In order to understand Carnell's ethical theory, as well as his practical work, it is necessary to understand his thinking on the concept of authority as it pertains to these topics. This chapter, then, will treat the meaning of authority in Carnell's thought, as well as the way Carnell viewed his authoritative text, the Bible--the role it played in his ethical thinking, and the degree to which he participated in the evangelical tradition of using the Bible as the authority for ethical statements.

The Meaning of Authority

No single definition of authority is held in common by all ethicists. A typical one, however, is the view that authority is the power to command or to force another. Yet this idea does not exhaust the concept of authority. Several other meanings of the term, which will be helpful in analyzing Carnell, can be distinguished.(1) Authority, for example can refer to one with superior knowledge in a particular field, and is known as epistemic authority. An epistemic moral authority has superior knowledge in the moral realm, such knowledge being of moral principles, moral reasoning, or conventional norms. Such authority need not be limited to a person; it may be a number of persons. A closely-related type of authority is exemplary moral authority, the type where the authority's behavior, rather than knowledge, is a model for others. Often values and attitudes are communicated most effectively by exemplary moral authority, whereas expertise in moral reasoning is best communicated through epistemic moral authority.(2) As in the case of epistemic moral authority, the influence exerted by an exemplary moral authority depends upon the degree of receptivity exercised by the authority's subjects. It should be noted that epistemic and exemplary moral authority, unlike the executive moral authority discussed initially, carry no right to command, and thus are completely dependent, as regards their effectiveness, upon the will of their subjects. This point casts light upon what appears to be a common element in all of these concepts of the meaning of authority. It has been noted that authority possesses a relational quality which is exhibited between the authority's bearer and its subject. In addition, no authority is an authority-in-general: it must be an authority related to a particular field. Outside of that field it is not an authority. "All authority is thus essentially a relation among a <u>bearer</u>, a <u>subject</u>, and a <u>field</u>, in virtue of a particular quality, attribute or context."(3) With these preliminary remarks in mind, we may begin an investigation of Carnell's thinking on authority.

Carnell asserts that any authority must meet two general criteria: (1)it must be trustworthy and credible, and (2)it must demonstrate an access to relevant data, so that when the authority's claims are tested, the subject's expectations are sustained.(4) We need to make two observations about Carnell's criteria. First, they show that his idea of authority comports with the above-stated common element in concepts of authority. If an authority is trustworthy, then it is a <u>bearer</u> of authority. If it demonstrates an access to relevant data, it concerns a particular <u>field</u>. For another's expectations to be sustained, a <u>subject</u> is necessitated. Second, the criteria show that Carnell has in mind a kind of authority which at least is epistemic. Such authority is derived from the knowledge possessed. It knows nothing of force or power. The extent of the authority possessed by the bearer depends upon the degree of receptivity offered by the subjects. That degree of receptivity is proportional to the trustworthiness of the bearer. It only takes a few cases of error on the part of the bearer for the subject to withdraw receptivity.(5) This, it will be noticed, is the very point Carnell is making. An authority must be trustworthy.

An epistemic authority also has to be able to transfer knowledge to the subjects. Private or secret knowledge has no place in this kind of authority.

> Epistemic authority is thus in principle substitutional in nature. Its purpose is to substitute the knowledge of one person in a certain field for the lack

of knowledge of another.. . .

> It is only because others can in fact acquire the knowledge of the bearer of epistemic authority that an epistemic authority can achieve the authority he has.(6)

This criterion has contained in it the need for the subject to have enough prior knowledge of the field to be able to test the authority's knowledge claims, in order to understand and acquire them for himself or herself. This, though, is the point of Carnell's second criterion: the authority has a knowledge which is laid before the subject for testing. From the point of view of the subject, Carnell describes authority this way: "A normal person does not submit his life to an authority until, guided by reason, he is fully assured in his mind that the authority in question is trustworthy."(7) Here we find repeated the same two criteria: a knowledge which can be tested by the subject (reason) and trustworthiness. It is thus safe to conclude that Carnell's concept of authority includes at least an epistemic authority.

The next question to ask is, what is the epistemic moral authority for Carnell? It was noted earlier that such an authority may be other than a person. Such is the case for Carnell. In at least three of his books he identifies the authority as the Bible. In one, on the subject of the Bible, he writes of "the spirit of authority and finality with which it speaks."(8) A second presents a stronger statement, defining orthodoxy as "that branch of Christendom which limits the ground of religious authority to the Bible."(9) A third statement, and one which hints at what Carnell holds to be the tools used by the subject to test the authority, is this.

> The conservative ardently defends a system of authority. It was the conviction of the coherence of Scripture's authority which touched off the Reformation. What the conservative does reject . . . is the notion that authoritative decree *per se*, unaccompanied by rational evidences of the authority, can be a basis for faith.(10)

A discussion of Carnell's concept of Scripture will come later. The point being made now is that for Carnell, Scripture, and Scripture alone, is the written epistemic moral authority.

The concept of epistemic moral authority does not exhaust Carnell's concept of authority, for Scripture is not autonomous; it is related to God. The epistemic authority of Scripture is derived from the divine authority of God.(11) Carnell joins the two by writing that Jesus taught that Scripture has the force of law and should be received on divine authority. Jesus, however, "received his doctrine from the Father," and thus "everything that Jesus says is true on divine authority."(12) Yet it appears that Carnell goes beyond epistemic authority when speaking of Jesus' teaching to a joining of that authority with exemplary authority. What Jesus says, along with all Biblical teaching, is epistemically authoritative, but "To conceive of the Bible as the primary revelation is heresy. If there had been no redemptive events, there would be no theology."(13) Scripture is the means by which an individual comes into contact with both the exemplary and epistemic authorities of Christ, for "in the one act of reading Scripture, we meet Christ in two complementary ways. <u>First</u>, we confront Christ's person.. . . <u>Secondly</u>, we receive a propositional revelation of Christ's will." Put simply, "The written Word is the locus of confrontation with the living Word."(14) What is this, though, but an assertion that the epistemic authority of Scripture is incomplete without the combined epistemic and exemplary authority of Jesus? It is, in fact, more than that. It is the claim that Scripture, while remaining a valid epistemic authority itself, is primarily a means to a higher level of authority: the epistemic and exemplary authority of Jesus. "Propositional revelation is an instrumental value; it is designed to bring us into fellowship with Jesus Christ."(15)

It has been previously stated that epistemic and exemplary authority carries no right, in itself, to force a subject into a particular action.(16) This point raises an immediate question. If these kinds of authority do not coerce, then what is their positive function as moral authorities? The answer lies in the presupposition that there is a knowable morality which can be communicated through principles, values, and ideals. It is because we desire to know and exhibit such morality that we employ the two kinds of authority in question. Epistemic moral authorities can communicate a possessed knowledge of the morality, and exemplary moral authorities so act as to display that same morality. That is their sole function.(17) As can be expected, Carnell accepts the presupposition of a transcendent reality. For him, "reality 'out there' is the truth."(18) In the moral realm, that reality is God's will. "For the will of God is the highest rule of justice; so that what he wills must be considered just for this very reason, because he wills it."(19) The morality taught and displayed by the epistemic and exemplary moral authorities, if it is to be legitimate, has to have this limit placed upon it: the morality's principles must serve the human interest.(20) Carnell agrees with this point. "All men know that whatever conduces to their well-being is the good.. . . " He goes on to join that idea to the previous one of a transcendent morality when he asks, "How is it that we are able confidently to say that what is good today will be good tomorrow, unless we lodge our theory of the good in something outside the process of history?"(21) That theory of good is precisely the knowable morality which the epistemic moral authority communicates and the exemplary moral authority demonstrates. Theirs is a teaching role. For Carnell, the teaching comes through Scripture. "The Christian avoids the flux of time and space by appealing to the mind of God Who has revealed Himself in Scripture." In Scripture one finds an epistemic authority, God's will,(22) as well as an exemplary authority, the life of Christ.(23)

Realizing that epistemic and exemplary moral authorities do not carry the right to enforce, we ask the obvious question: what does? To answer this question in the light of Carnell's thinking, we must determine the extent to which God is required in Carnell's discussion of ethics. This is nothing else but the question of the relationship of theology and ethics. The most widely held answer has been that theology and ethics need not be inseparably linked. Reinhold Niebuhr, for example, wrote

> Christian thought has consistently maintained that the law must be regarded, not simply as something which is given man either by revelation, or

> for that matter by the authority of
> society, but as written in the heart.
> This can only mean that the requirements
> of action, dictated by man's essential
> nature, are a part of his real self.(24)

There are those, however, who hold the opposite view. An example is William of Ockham, who held that ethical propositions are true only because of a divine act.(25) It is into this second camp that Carnell falls. In his A Philosophy of the Christian Religion he writes,

> Without ethics we have bestiality in the
> most viscious form; but without
> metaphysics as a foundation for ethics,
> bestiality remains. Ethical insights
> are grounded in metaphysical values.(26)

In fact, without metaphysics, ethics has no understandable content, for "ethical propositions have cognitive meaning only when they rest in metaphysical ultimates."(27) For Carnell, the metaphysical ultimate is God, for God is the standard of good. "Good ethics are derived from God.. . . [A] society is properly ordered only when it does the will of God."(28)

What is it that convinces Carnell that good ethics are derived from God? He begins the answer by assuming that all people must act. When a person chooses a course of conduct, that choice reveals the fact that the person is committed to a particular value. The question the person must ask is, "To what am I committed as I act?" What is it that gives meaning to my actions? Upon reflection the person will realize that he is committed to the law of justice. When offended, he judges the offender guilty. His judicial sentiment is aroused automatically. He cannot control that part of himself which demands justice.

> We have no part in either the arousing
> or the subduing of the judicial
> sentiment. The entire transaction
> occurs without authorization from our
> will.. . . We have no power to awaken
> it, and we have no power to placate
> it.(29)

We live in a moral and spiritual environment which requires our inner beings to demand justice. We cannot escape the environment, and so cannot escape the requirement. What is that environment? It is God. ". . . The person of God forms the moral and spiritual environment in which man lives and moves and is.. . . Man subsists in God from the first moment of moral self-consciousness . . ."(30) Carnell defines the same environment in a second way. He writes, "We live and move and have our being in a transcendental realm of values."(31) Carnell drew theology and morality together by asserting that they both are definitions of the same thing: that in which we live and move and have our being. For Carnell, to speak of the ethical realm is tantamount to speaking of the theological realm. The reality is the same. Only the terminology is different.

This point is vital for an understanding of Carnell's discussion of duty. Without it as a basis, statements such as this one make no sense: "Duty is never experienced until one stands in the center of duty; and one can only do this by submitting to the claims of the moral and spiritual environment."(32) Yet, by realizing that for Carnell the one reality is described by two different vocabularies, the moral realm is never experienced until a person submits to the claims of God upon his moral life. "Were it not that we live and move and are in God, we should not know what duty is." That submission comes through a humbling of self before the God whose character constitutes him as the moral guardian of the individual, one made in God's image. The individual is "made like God" in that he or she shares God's attribute of justice. He or she lives in an environment of transcendent values, one which is given substance by the person of God. By humbly submitting to God's person, an individual can understand the values to which the attribute of justice within him or her points when offended by another person. "We demand justice because we live and move and are in God." The person's desire for justice when offended by another is God directly working. "Justice pertains to the administration of the right, and God's image in man is the fixed point for defining this administration.. . . God judges him through us."(33)

Who is the God in whom we live and move and exist, and how may we submit to him? Having relized the moral commitment in which he has been involved from the first moment of self-consciousness, that of the law of justice, how may the individual know more completely the duties laid upon him by God, the moral and spiritual environment? Carnell answers by defining his God:

> the Christian's major premise is not just an appeal to a good God; rather it is to the God who has revealed Himself in Scripture, and to Him alone.(34)

Why? It is because "nothing is duty unless it captures the heart as a command."(35) For Carnell, that means an appeal to epistemic and exemplary moral authority. The commands of the decalogue are the duties laid upon the individual by God, both in relation to God and in relation to others,(36) and the life of Christ shows that fellowship with God is life's primary value.(37) What Carnell has done is to make epistemic and exemplary moral authorities means by which the individual may come in contact with the executive moral authority, God, in whom he has his moral existence.

Carnell's theory of obligation is the kind of rule deontology known as the Divine Command theory, the view which holds that the standard of right and wrong is God's will or God's law.(38) "The Christian says that the will of God is the final standard of good, and that what God wills is good because he wills it."(39) Divine Command theory asserts that God's commandment is what makes an action right or wrong. In Carnell's thinking, this assertion is seen in his appeal to the epistemic moral authority of Scripture as the basis for discerning the duties of the moral and spiritual environment.

There may be an egoistic element to the Divine Command theory, and in Carnell's thinking such is the case. He appealed to human desire when defending his assertion that the individual should submit to the epistemic moral authority of Scripture.

> God achieves a perfect union of duty and desire by means of a legitimate system of rewards and punishments. The duty of man is to do God's will. The desire is to have happiness and life. In Christianity these are united, for God gives happiness and life to all who do His will. This is the affirmative

> incentive for proper duty to God.. . .
>
> The <u>negative</u> incentive for proper duty to God is the pain which God inflicts upon all who spurn His offer of reconciliation.(40)

In addition to his claim that an act's goodness is determined by the content of divine command, Carnell seeks to motivate the individual to submit to God's authority by arguing that to do so is merely to act in his own interest. An element of teleology is thus apparent in Carnell's Divine Command theory.

The Meaning of Scripture

For Carnell, to speak of God's authority is to speak of the Word of God. Christ, the exemplary moral authority, is the living Word of God, and the Bible, the epistemic moral authority, is the written Word of God.(41) The Bible is God's coming to man; it is not the liberal notion of man's coming to God.(42) As such, it is that particular type of revelation in which God discloses himself. That self-disclosure is the unique characteristic which warrants for the Bible the term <u>special</u> revelation.(43) The body of writing which Carnell accepts as "the Bible" is "not part or piece, but the full and whole sixty-six canonical books."(44) Apart from these books there is no written Word of God.(45)

When confronted with the fact that no original autographs of these books are extant, and the question of how our current Bible is related to those original writings, Carnell readily admits that today's English versions, as well as the extant transcriptions of the autographs, contain scribal errors. Yet he is quick to state also that these errors are of minimal significance.

> What we possess in our present Bibles today is a remarkably substantial copy of the first set of writings . . . the present text is in a state of substantial purity . . . the copyists were providentially preserved from disturbing the doctrinal content of Scripture.(46)

Convinced that ongoing research increasingly substantiates his positon, Carnell adds, "The more dirt the spade of the archaeologist turns over, the more harmonious becomes our knowledge of the text."(47)

Carnell is careful to place his view of Scripture between a neo-orthodox view and what he labels "an odious Biblicism." Presumably this latter position is Carnell's impression of fundamentalism, while the former is represented, in Carnell's mind, by Reinhold Niebuhr.(48) His mediating position is that "The Bible is the Word of God 'out there,' whether or not anyone is confronted by it." Yet, remaining true to his view of Scripture as an authority which requires the epistemic and exemplary moral authority of Jesus, he adds that the Bible "does not address the heart as the Word of God until Christ is met in personal fellowship. The living Word is the soul of the written Word."(49)

Carnell asserts the inerrancy and infallibility of the inspired Scripture. For him, "Scripture contains the only infallible rule of faith and practice."(50) Inspiration means "moved by the Holy Spirit to write down only what God approved,"(51) and inerrant inspiration means that each element of Scripture is coherent with everything else in Scripture. The Bible contains no logical or historical mistakes. Such inspiration is a characteristic only of the original autographs. Setting himself against the neo-orthodox position again, Carnell questions the view that the Biblical writers were mere witnesses to God's working in history, holding rather that God superintended their work.(52) It is with disapproval that he explains Niebuhr's self-understanding as a Biblical realist.

> The Bible is not God's objective revelation, . . . as in orthodoxy; for science, according to Niebuhr, has forever smashed plenary inspiration. The Bible is a very fallible document penned by very human authors.(53)

Since the Bible, according to Carnell's viewpoint, is an inerrant unity of divinely-superintended writings, it follows that Carnell asserts that the Bible is a system of truth.(54) The one criterion by which the system must be tested is that of systematic consistency, the law of contradiction.(55) He sees that the Bible meets the criterion, since it is "internally consistent."(56) It must be judged as a whole, however, or it will appear to be naive or inadequate. Suffering, for example, is an offense to partiality. But whole perspective sees in suffering a <u>conditio sine qua non</u> for the acquisition of all worthwhile things. Carnell is not willing to assert that the Bible, as a whole system, is a complete system. He sees that it contains many blind spots. Yet its characteristic which warrants its acceptance by the rational individual is that it presents a system "which is attended by the fewest difficulties."(57) Scripture is not a finished system, but merely one which is outlined.(58) Its system of propositions "addresses the reason as decisively as any other faculty in man."(59)

Carnell attacks Niebuhr concerning Scripture as a whole system. He argues that Niebuhr makes the mistake of using Scripture only at those places where it is dialectical. Non-dialectical truth, according to Niebuhr, is not outside the realm of immanence. Therefore, it is not necessary to consult the Bible in non-dialectical matters. Niebuhr makes the mistake of judging the Bible by dialectical insights; orthodoxy properly judges dialectical insights by the entire system of Biblical propositions.(60)

It should be pointed out that in Carnell's biblical system all verses are not equally normative. One basic element of this idea is that "<u>in no case does the Old Testament enjoy primacy over the New Testament.</u>" Carnell is quick to point out, however, that "the New Testament <u>fulfills</u> the Old Testament; it does not reject it."(61) Not even all parts of the New Testament are equally normative, though. The biblical system, for Carnell, is the content of Romans and Galatians, for only they present Christian truth in systematic, didactic form.(62) This principle of New Testament supremacy is carried directly into the realm of ethics. ". . . [T]he New Testament ethic judges the truncated ethic of the Old Testament." Jesus' love commandment is a new commandment, not merely a summary of the decalogue. The ten commandments are no better than the ethic of Plato and Aristotle, while the New Testament ethic stands in judgment on them all.(63)

What emerges from this concept of superior or primary parts of Scripture is the question of hermeneutics. In general, Carnell's position is the

Reformed one, in which Scripture interprets itself. The primary tool of study is exegesis.(64) In answer to charges, such as Niebuhr's, that this approach is too literal,(65) Carnell writes, "If orthodoxy is literalistic because it honors the rights of language in Scripture, it is in very good company, for Christ and the apostles approach the text in precisely the same manner."(66) That literalism and honoring of the rights of language he summarizes in five rules of hermeneutics:

> <u>First</u>, the New Testament interprets the Old Testament; <u>secondly</u>, the Epistles interpret the Gospels; <u>thirdly</u>, systematic passages interpret the incidental; <u>fourthly</u>, universal passages interpret the local; <u>fifthly</u>, didactic passages interpret the symbolic. If any rule is neglected, the harmony of Scripture is disrupted.(67)

Presumably this last sentence refers to Carnell's idea of a Scriptural system. The result of this approach to Scripture is that "the voice of God is heard in the heart through the pages of the Holy Bible."(68) This approach to Scripture which views it as God's message to humanity concurs with Carnell's view of God as the executive moral authority and the Bible as the epistemic moral authority through which the individual may come into contact with the demands of God.

Since Carnell is convinced that ongoing scholarship only increases the wealth of evidence that substantiates his view of the Biblical text, it follows that he would affirm the value of lower criticism. This he does while distinguishing his scholarly position from the intellectually-bankrupt view held by fundamentalism.(69) He is not so eager to accept higher criticism, however, for he sees that the higher critic's philosophy of reality is at odds with that of the orthodox Christian. The former views reality naturally and mechanically, while the latter views it supernaturalistically and redemptively. The former assumes there has been no divine revelation; the latter assumes that there has been.(70) Higher critics, according to Carnell, do not destroy the evangelical view of Scripture's inspiration; rather, they biasly presuppose against it. Their problem is not one of facts, but of attitude.(71) The higher critic comes to the biblical text with the same scientific methods as are used on other books. He or she presupposes that the Bible is merely a human production to which the scientific method may be applied. What he or she fails to realize is that such a presupposition violates the biblical message concerning itself.(72) It is because of its presuppositions, not its conclusions, that Carnell characterizes higher criticism as destructive,(73) although he does note that "It is only <u>destructive</u> higher criticism against which the conservative argues, a method which <u>corrects</u>, rather than interprets the Bible."(74) Presumably he meant that he would affirm higher criticism at those points where its conclusions concur with his own.

It remains for us to investigate Carnell's general idea on how the authority of Scripture is related to ethics. His most basic assertion is that biblical Christianity affirms those values which all individuals, by nature, seek.(75) The Bible, being from God and free from error, contains all that is necessary for both faith (religion) and practice (morality). God has revealed his will in the Bible, and Christians have a moral responsibility to follow that system of revealed truth.(76) What Carnell asserts obviously is a case of divine command theory; yet we also see in his assertion a Carnellian idea which appeared in the theoretical discussion of authority: the theological realm is the same reality as the ethical realm; only the language varies. It is only with this idea in mind that Carnell's statement avoids the naturalistic fallacy: ". . . how can we know what the character of all reality is, so as to act wisely, unless God tells us? . . . Revelation, then, is a condition <u>sine qua non</u> for our soul's well-being."(77) When we make such a submission to the biblical teaching, we experience nothing which is offensive to our moral tastes. Rather, we find that the biblical truth offers the highest moral experience.(78) When challenged with a morally-offensive biblical incident such as the Amalekite massacre, Carnell responded with an appeal to progressive revelation. Israel's war tactics were no more cruel than the prevailing standard. Those tactics God used to accomplish his will, not because Israel's insensitivity to God prevented it from implementing merciful standards. Not until after the ministry of Jesus could God's people understand those weightier matters of the law.(79)

The Use of Scripture in Ethics

Carnell's emphasis upon the Bible as the supreme authoritative text for ethics automatically raises the question of how Scripture is to be used in ethics. In treating Carnell's view on this question, we encounter the same problem as we had in approaching his eschatology: nowhere does he deal with the subject in a systematic fashion. From his position on the nature of Scripture we would suspect that his uses, no matter what they may be, would be authoritative in an absolute sense. This, in fact, is the case. Carnell allows no place for Jack T. Sanders' useless-for-modern-ethics approach to Scripture,(80) nor does he employ the somewhat authoritative view of James M. Gustafson.(81) Instead, Carnell uses the Bible as both an absolute and final authority. It is supremely applicable to the present situation in a way in which no other authority is applicable, and it is not merely one of a list of authorities which inform ethical decisions. When the Bible speaks, it is to be believed and followed, irrespective of the input offered by other authorities. The Bible does not speak in only one way, however. Carnell's uses of Scripture depend largely upon two factors: his audience and his subject matter.

Following some of his evangelical predecessors, Carnell sees in the Bible an over-arching theme which is to control Christian ethics. In Matt. 16:26 he finds the theme of the worth of human life lived under the lordship of Christ. As a system of values, Christianity is built around this theme. In all of his striving, the Christian is to seek to inculcate this theme in his life and in the lives of others. Such inculcation cannot be forced, however, for lordship is a result of trust and submission. If an individual, upon reflection, does not realize his need to adopt this theme as the controlling element in his life, no amount of logical demonstration will persuade him or her.(82) All of the other uses of Scripture are aimed at producing and maintaining this lordship of Christ in both the individual and the society which seek to live by this theme.

One use of Scripture which Carnell used predominantly, though not exclusively, when addressing an evangelical audience was to see in the Bible eternal, transcendent truth to be applied to particular cultures and issues. Doctrine was drawn out of the Bible in a literal fashion, and was then used to color the viewpoint taken on particular questions. In <u>An Introduction to Christian Apologetics</u>, while discussing the basis for asserting that murder is wrong, he cited a verse which teaches that people are made in God's image. Because of that fact, he concluded that an individual is God's special property and ought not to be murdered. It is particularly because of this theological fact, rather than society's norms, personal interest, or convenience that Carnell adopted his position and sought to convince others of the same.(83)

In April of 1951 Carnell published an article in <u>His</u> magazine, an evangelical publication for college students. In that article he discussed the question of whether a Christian, in light of Jesus' teaching not to resist evil, should go to war for his or her country. He argued from Rom. 13 that government is ordained by God as the agent which prevents anarchy in society. It, along with the home and church, are the three spheres in which the Christian is to live. He went on to explain that the way government fulfills its divinely-sanctioned task is to restrain forcefully those who desire to do evil (Rom. 13:4). From these verses he concluded that, as one who lives in the sphere of government, the Christian is to participate in war if that war serves to check wrong-doers.(84)

> If one will clear his mind and recognize the full implications of Scripture, he will see that this observation (about the three spheres) contains the solution to the problem of war . . .; as one officially delegated by the state to execute the decree of judgment against those who refuse to stay within the bounds of justice, he trips the lever which opens the bomb door effecting the instant death of a hundred thousand people.(85)

The one major instance in which Carnell employs Scripture in this way (that is, as transcendent truth to be applied to particular cultures and issues) when addressing an audience which is not largely evangelical occurs in his article, "A Christian Social Ethics," written in 1963 for <u>The Christian Century</u>. Here he applied the doctrine of the lordship of Christ, as found in 2 Cor. 10:5, to the social sphere, concluding that since the initial act of personal salvation required the lordship of Christ, so should all subsequent acts undertaken by the Christian. Those acts include, of course, the founding of Sunday schools and missions, but they also include the pursuit of justice in society.(86)

Another of Carnell's uses of Scripture is to find contained therein a divinely-revealed morality in the form of commands or laws. This use is quite similar to one of Carl Henry's uses,(87) in that it sees the motivation for obeying God's laws as being love. For Carnell, the one who loves has fulfilled the law, even to the point of keeping specific commandments, for love does no wrong to a neighbor, which is the point of the commandments. He quoted Rom. 18:8-10 to support his position.(88) Like Henry, however, Carnell did not take his position to antinomianism, but maintained that love means keeping commandments. Applying his view to the moral realm, he quoted Jesus' words as recorded in John 14:15, "If you love me, you will keep my commandments," and concluded, "Christianity therefore, instead of removing the motive for moral struggle, offers the highest reason for exterminating evil."(89)

Two examples will serve to demonstrate how Carnell employed Scripture as divinely-revealed moral commands or laws when dealing with specific issues. In his article, "Is Drunkenness A Sin?," he answered his own question for his evangelical audience by a direct condemnation, based upon 1 Cor. 6:9-10. He further drew from the verses a judgment of eternal damnation upon the drunkard, for, according to Carnell, the drunkard has spurned God's law.(90) The use is just this simple. The question is asked, and a passage of Scripture is quoted in response.

Carnell employed this use of Scripture in a positive way in "Should A Christian Go to War?" Previously he had found in the first part of Rom. 13 a general truth which he applied to the question. This time, however, he found in the first two verses of Rom. 13 a direct command which, he contended, was the Christian's responsibility to obey.

> . . . the Christian is under solemn command from God to respond as a good citizen to the obligations placed upon

> him by the ruling authorities. He is to
> be obedient to the government in all
> ways except those which involve a
> transgression of the law of God.(91)

It should be pointed out that occasionally Carnell employed a perversion of these previous two uses of Scripture known as the proof-text. This use of the Bible wrenches a sentence or phrase from its cultural and historical context and applies it to a situation to which it was not originally applicable. It is true that other uses make applications which were not originally intended, but the unique characteristic of the proof-text use is that its user makes such applications by virtue of the fact that the text is not viewed as a part of a greater whole. Rather, the text is viewed autonomously, transcending its cultural and historical cradle. Carnell appears to have reserved this use exclusively for evangelical audiences. At one point in "The Christian and Television" he made the point that the Christian must realize the need for relaxation, for not only is he under great social pressure, but he, of all people, realizes the constant warfare between good and evil. Then, applying the proof-text use, he concluded that because of both the pressure and the realization, the Christian will "weep night and day with tears" for the salvation of individuals. This phrase is taken from Acts 20, a chapter which records Paul's final address to the leaders of the church at Ephesus. In verse 31 the apostle reminds the leaders that for three years he warned them, night and day, with tears, about those who would try to destroy the church. It is plain that Carnell used this verse without regard for its historical setting when he applied it to modern Christians, living within a constant struggle between good and evil, showing concern for the salvation of individuals.(92)

Carnell asserted in <u>Christian Commitment: An Apologetic</u>, that the person of character has more moral responsibilities than he has resources to fulfill. Each social situation presents an infinite task. As an illustration of his point, Carnell mentioned the man, for example, who boards a bus. At that moment he has to make the choice between helping a woman with her groceries, giving his seat to an elderly man, or offering a word of wise advice to a boy. He cannot do all, and may even do nothing. Why? "The spirit indeed is willing, but the flesh is weak." In the previous example Carnell offered a mild suggestion regarding a proper Christian response; in this example he offered an explanation of a probable response of any upright person. In both examples he used Scripture as proof-text, yet in different ways. The second text, taken from Matthew's account of Jesus talking to his disciples in Gethsemane just prior to his crucifixion, described the disciples' inability to stay awake while Jesus prayed. Obviously, Carnell took no account of this fact when applying the text to a man getting on a bus.(93)

Another use Carnell made of Scripture, following in the evangelical tradition, was to use Biblical figures as moral examples for present Christians. Not all of these figures were positive models as, say, Paul. In "Is Drunkenness A Sin?," he used Noah as a model not to be followed: "One of the most odious social evils which has plagued men since Noah had that little winefest inside his tent, is the sin of drunkenness." The prodigal son was also used as a warning-model for Christians.(94) Yet most of the times Carnell employed this use, it was in a positive sense. Since this use is slightly more liberal than the previous uses, we would expect to find it in the writings where Carnell appealed to an audience which was not primarily evangelical. Such is the case. In his <u>Christian Century</u> article, "A Christian Social Ethics" he employed this use more than any other, and in his <u>Christian Economics</u> article, "Personal Happiness and Prosperity," this use predominated. Interestingly, we find one of the negative models in this article. While arguing that a mere increase in possessions will not bring an increase in happiness, Carnell cited an experience from the life of King Ahab (1 Kings 21) in which the king, already rich, coveted his neighbor's field. When the neighbor refused to surrender the field, the king returned so depressed that he would not eat. Carnell's point was that the king, rather than remembering and using what he had, desired what he did not have, thinking that it would make him happy. The result was the opposite. Christians who seek to be happy should avoid following the example of the king.(95)

As would be expected, Carnell's foremost moral model was the life of Christ., In this same article, for example, Jesus' life is used as a model of the happiest ever lived. Noting that Christ was little concerned with the things that typically capture an individual's attention (career, real estate, money) Carnell made the point that Jesus, having his life fulfilled in God, did not view material possessions as the key to happiness. He extrapolated from this example the fact that American prosperity was not an infallible sign of a well-integrated social order. Christians would do well to follow Christ's example, seeking to share things rather than to own them.(96)

In the ethics chapter of <u>An Introduction to Christian Apologetics</u>, while discussing duty and desire, Carnell argued that desire must be restrained by duty. His biblical support was the Old Testament example of Joseph who, when invited to join Potiphar's wife in a sexual act which was not lawful, "left his garment in her hand, and fled, and got him out" (Gen. 39:12, KJV). Joseph knew God's law, which was the basis of duty, and acted in such a way as to fulfill his duty, though it conflicted with his desire. "An ethical man learns to say <u>no</u> under many circumstances, for the very reason that <u>he</u> discovers a discrepancy between what he desires to do and what he ought to do."(97)

There remains but one Carnellian use of Scripture in normative ethics. As was the case with Andrew R. Osborn,(98) Carnell saw in the Bible general ethical principles which were to be applied in specific situations. Differing from Osborn, however, Carnell did not see lists of rules, such as the Ten Commandments merely as embodiments of the principles which were applicable only to the cultures which produced them. In this point he is closer to Henry, holding that, in areas where there are no specific Biblical instructions, the principle must be applied.

Osborn felt that the dominant principle was justice. Carnell appears to have supported this viewpoint. At one point in "A Christian Social Ethics" he made the point that since the gospel and social justice are moral correlatives, it is the responsibility of the Christian to support every action which furthers the cause of justice. In fact, concern for justice is a clear indication that an individual has experienced the transforming love of Christ. The one who claims to be a Christian, yet downgrades justice, offends God. The prophet Ezekiel stated the principle this way: "Thus says the Lord God.... Put away violence and oppression, and execute justice and righteousness . . ." (Ezek. 45:9, RSV). When the conservative gets disturbed when he or she observes the liberal neglecting the gospel in favor of the promotion of justice, according to Carnell he or she should remember that it is equally disturbing to God to see the conservative neglecting the promotion of justice while proclaiming the gospel.(99)

Throughout his writings, Carnell employed a number of biblical moral principles. Not all of them can be explained and illustrated here. Yet two more are significant to warrant expansion. The first may roughly be viewed as a principle of consideration. When an individual is unjustly accused, embarrassed, or ridiculed, that person deserves an apology from the offending person. To avoid becoming the offending party, an individual should follow the advice of Paul, "Give no offense to Jews or to Greeks or to the church of God" (1 Cor. 10:32, RSV). Put simply, a person should be courteous. When a person is offended by another, the response should not be one of wrath or revenge, but the principle of consideration should be applied. The offended party should follow the advice of Paul in Eph. 4:31-32, and forgive the one who has offended. For Carnell, this principle was capsulized in Matt. 7:12, and was viewed as a summary of the law and the prophets.(100)

Carnell found a scriptural principle which, in reality, was a restatement of the over-arching theme which colored all of his employment of the Bible in ethics: the lordship of Christ. At the end of "The Christian and Television," he took his standard mediating position, asserting that with respect to television the Christian must be vigilant, avoiding both complacency and negativism. Using Col. 3:17, he stated this principle:

> The rule of the Christian life is healthy and balanced: Whether we eat or drink (or watch television) we are to do all to the glory of God with thanksgiving.(101)

The preceding list includes all of Carnell's major uses of the Bible in normative ethics. Yet there remains one use which occurs exclusively, with one possible exception, in <u>Christian Commitment: An Apologetic</u>. Carnell's approach was to acquaint the individual with the moral and spiritual environment in which he lived by looking at his personal moral experiences and by asking what it was that gave them meaning. He used the Bible in this exercise as an interpretive and analytical tool. The answers to the questions which arose as a result of seeking to make sense out of personal experience could be found in Scripture. Several examples will help clarify this use as one distinct from the others.

In discussing the judicial sentiment, that human moral faculty which is automatically offended when one person is wronged by another, Carnell argued that every normal person, as a result of reflecting upon his or her own moral make-up, will discover an inner sense of personal worth and dignity. As the individual continues reflecting a natural question will arise: "Why do I have a sense of my own personal worth and dignity?" The answer is found in the fact that "no man ever hates his own flesh, but nourishes and cherishes it, as Christ does the church" (Eph. 5:29, RSV). Immediately after quoting this verse, Carnell added, "God has ensured that a man of character will never take a light view of the image of God in him." What Carnell did was to interpret the verse ("The person, who bears the divine image, will love his body in the same way that Christ loves the church. He has no choice in the matter."), and then use it as an analytical tool in answering the original question.(102)

Later on in the book Carnell observed that the normal person will realize that he or she is finite, depending upon powers greater than himself or herself. These powers center in God, who grants everything as a gracious gift. This realization should prompt the reflective person to spontaneous sentiments of gratitude. Yet, if the person is honest, he or she will realize that though the desire for those sentiments is present, the power to make the desire a reality is not. The natural question becomes "Why?" Carnell interpreted this situation by quoting Jer. 13:23 (RSV): "Can the Ethiopian change his skin or the leopard his spots? Then also you can do good who are accustomed to do evil." His point was that it is impossible for the individual to change into a spontaneously-thankful person, for an evil person (which we all are, by nature) cannot become good by self effort. The more moral we try to become, the less moral we end up, for our attempts (calculated actions) conflict with the goal (spontaneity). The result is the moral predicament.

> Although it is evil to be morally indifferent to those who do us favors, not only are we not held by a spontaneous sense of gratitude when we contemplate the divine favors, but we have insufficient moral resources to convert ourselves.

Thus not only did Carnell use a verse as a basis for interpreting the question which resulted from self-observation and reflection, but he extrapolated from it a basic descriptive statement which he subsequently applied to all parallel human experience. All people, he concluded, would struggle with this fact in their lives.(103)

Carnell did not employ this use only when dealing with questions of being or responses, but extended its application to questions resulting from action. Any person, he contended, will have his or her moral peace upset if he or she neglects the duty to save a life by an act in the interest of the other, not in the interest of self. The natural tendency, however, is to act in self-interest. The reflective person will normally ask this question: "Why do I become more insecure when I act so as to further my own security?" Carnell answered with a verse which he considered to be applicable in all human situations at all times: "Whoever seeks to gain his life will lose it, but whoever loses his life will preserve it" (Luke 17:33, RSV). This verse reveals a truth which is basic to the human condition; nothing can change it. The reason why a person becomes more insecure after acting in a way to further personal security is that that person has not acted out of love for neighbor. That action offends God, who responds by disturbing the moral peace of the individual. The individual feels insecure. Again, Carnell has used a verse to analyze a situation which, he asserts, will sound familiar to anyone who reflects upon his or her own experience.(104)

It is obvious that Carnell adopted no specific viewpoint on the question of the use of Scripture in ethics. Whereas in The Case for Orthodox Theology he has a chapter on hermeneutics, presumably this is intended, as the title would suggest, for the theological realm. In contrast, he has no treatment of the question from a theoretical point of view. We search Carnell's writings in vain for a section on hermeneutics for ethics. If, then, a theoretical orientation did not guide his use of Scripture in ethics, what did?

The controlling motivating factor in most of Carnell's work was apologetics. His goal was to develop convincing arguments for the adoption of orthodox Protestantism. Since Carnell did not assume a static approach to his task, this goal, rather than a prior conviction regarding the proper approach to apologetics, colored his work.

> There is no 'official' or 'normative' approach to apologetics. At least I have never found one. The approach is governed by the climate of the times. This means, as it were, that an apologist must play it by ear.(105)

The result was that the same goal was approached from a number of different academic directions. In the preface to The Kingdom of Love and the Pride of Life Carnell wrote,

> In my own books on apologetics I have consistently tried to build upon some useful point of contact between the gospel and culture. In An Introduction to Christian Apologetics the appeal was to the law of contradiction; in A Philosophy of the Christian Religion it was to values; and in Christian Commitment it was to the judicial sentiment. In this book I am appealing to the law of love.(106)

Carnell realized that one type of argument, no matter how soundly it may be constructed, will not convince all audiences or individuals. The argument must be tailored for the predispositions and biases of its recipients. It was with this in mind that Carnell developed a multi-dimensional apologetics.

53

Carnell's ethical concern was closely parallel to his general apologetic concern: he sought to develop arguments for his ethical positions which would convince his readers. His uses of Scripture in ethics were tools which he felt would aid him in the achievement of his goal. The methodological question regarding Scripture was overshadowed and even displaced by the goal. It is for this reason that we find no systematic treatment of the issue of ethical hermeneutics in Carnell's writing, and why also we find no single use of Scripture in his argument.

The last point can be illustrated by observing the relationship between use and audience. The conservative uses (viewing the Bible as truth to be applied to ethics, revealed morality or commands or law, and proof-text) were employed when addressing an evangelical audience. They are found in An Introduction to Christian Apologetics, Christian Commitment: An Apologetic, and in articles published in United Evangelical Action, His, and Eternity. On rare occasions this use is found in an article published in The Christian Century or Christian Economics. The more liberal uses, however, are found when Carnell addressed a largely non-evangelical audience. The Bible used as moral example or principles is found in these latter two periodicals much more than are the former uses. The only reason for this is that Carnell's attempt was to build each argument with the goal of convincing a specific readership.

FOOTNOTES

(1) A more extensive treatment of each of these meanings can be found in Richard T. De George, "Authority and Morality," Frederick J. Adelmann, S.J., ed., *Authority* (The Hague, Netherlands: Martinus Nijhoff, 1974), pp. 31-49.

(2) De George, pp. 38-39. 41-42.

(3) Richard T. De George, "The Nature and Function of Epistemic Authority," R. Bine Harris, ed., *Authority: A Philosophical Analysis* (University: The Univ. of Alabama Press, 1976), p. 77.

(4) Edward John Carnell, *A Philosophy of the Christian Religion* (Grand Rapids: Eerdmans, 1960), p. 30.

(5) De George, "The Nature and Function of Epistemic Authority," p. 85.

(6) Ibid., p. 82.

(7) Edward John Carnell, *An Introduction to Christian Apologetics* (Grand Rapids: Eerdmans, 1949), p. 73.

(8) Carnell, *A Philosophy of the Christian Religion*, p. 30.

(9) Edward John Carnell, *The Case for Orthodox Theology* (Philadelphia: The Westminster Press, 1959), p. 33.

(10) Carnell, *An Introduction to Christian Apologetics*, p. 7.

(11) The issue of the meaning of divine authority will be treated later.

(12) Carnell, *The Case for Orthodox Theology*, pp. 36, 40, 41.

(13) Ibid., p. 49.

(14) Ibid., p. 34.

(15) Ibid., p. 48.

(16)This point has been argued by Richard T. De George in "The Nature and Function of Epistemic Authority."

(17)De George, "Authority and Morality," p. 46.

(18)Carnell, A Philosophy of the Christian Religion, p. 453.

(19)Edward John Carnell, Christian Commitment: An Apologetic (New York: Macmillan, 1957), p. 278.

(20)W. H. Werkmeister, "The Function and Limits of Moral Authority," R. Baine Harris, ed., Authority: A Philosophical Analysis (University: The University of Alabama Press, 1976), p. 98.

(21)Carnell, An Introduction to Christian Apologetics, p. 153.

(22)Ibid., pp. 328, 329.

(23)Carnell, A Philosophy of the Christian Religion, p. 452.

(24)Reinhold Niebuhr, The Nature and Destiny of Man, Vol. I, Human Nature (New York: Charles Scribner's Sons, 1964), pp. 274-275.

(25)Richard B. Brandt, Ethical Theory: The Problems of Normative and Critical Ethics (Englewood Cliffs: Prentice-Hall, Inc., 1959), p. 66.

(26)Carnell, A Philosophy of the Christian Religion, p. 177.

(27)Ibid., pp. 162-163.

(28)Carnell, An Introduction to Christian Apologetics, pp. 300, 312.

(29)Carnell, Christian Commitment: An Apologetic, pp. 36, 136, 172.

(30)Ibid., p. 101.

(31)Carnell, A Philosophy of the Christian Religion, pp. 177-178.

(32)Carnell, Christian Commitment: An Apologetic, p. 186.

(33)Ibid., pp. 126, 132, 133, 173.

(34)Carnell, An Introduction to Christian Apologetics, p. 177.

(35)Carnell, Christian Commitment: An Apologetic, p. 20.

(36)Carnell, An Introduction to Christian Apologetics, p. 331; Carnell, A Philosophy of the Christian Religion, p. 227.

(37)Carnell, A Philosophy of the Christian Religion, p. 277.

(38)Deontological theories assert that there may be considerations other than the goodness or badness of consequences which determine the rightness or wrongness of an act or rule. Rule deontology holds that the standard of rightness or wrongness consists of one or more rules. For a more detailed explanation of deontology, see William K. Frankena, Ethics (2d ed.; Englewood Cliffs: Prentice-Hall, Inc., 1973), pp. 14-17, 23-33.

(39)Carnell, A Philosophy of the Christian Religion, p. 313.

(40)Carnell, An Introduction to Christian Apologetics, pp. 331-332.

(41)Ibid., p. 199.

(42)Edward John Carnell, The Theology of Reinhold Neibuhr (revised ed., Grand Rapids: Eerdmans, 1960), p. 15.

(43)Edward John Carnell, "A Layman's Dictionary of Theology," Christian Herald, LXXXIII (July 1960), pp. 57-58. In his discussion of values and the necessity of revelation (An Introduction to Christian Apologetics, pp. 155-157), Carnell states that

> all insight into truth is an illumination by God of the heart, be

> that insight that two times two are four or that the grape is a fruit of the genera *Vitis* and *Muscadinia*.. . . Revelation, then, is simply the disclosure by God of truth which was previously unknown. Truth is seen in light and this light is from God.. . . Without revelation, there is no truth; for revelation is the light in which we see light.

Special revelation, however, is limited to that body of truth concerning *himself* which God discloses.

    (44)Carnell, *An Introduction to Christian Apologetics*, p. 174.

    (45)Carnell, *The Case for Orthodox Theology*, p. 33.

    (46)Carnell, *An Introduction to Christian Apologetics*, pp. 192-193.

    (47)Ibid., p. 193.

    (48)Carnell, *The Case for Orthodox Theology*, p. 33. Carnell's understanding of the neo-orthodox view of the Bible, and the one part from which he seeks to establish himself, is summarized in these statements from his *The Theology of Reinhold Niebuhr*, revised ed. "For . . . Niebuhr, therefore, the Bible is authoritative only at those points where there shines through a clarification of an experience gained earlier.. . . It is . . . the record of those events in history in which faith discerns the self-disclosure of God." (pp. 57, 120) (quote from *Human Nature*). The fundamentalist's position is described by Carnell in *The Case for Orthodox Theology*: ". . . the fundamentalist promptly concludes that everything worth knowing is in the Bible . . . he identifies *possession of the Word of God* with *possession of virtue*." (pp. 119, 125). It is between these extremes that Carnell places himself.

    (49)Carnell, *The Case for Orthodox Theology*, pp. 33, 34.

    (50)Edward John Carnell, "Conservatives and Liberals Do Not Need Each Other," Ronald H. Nash, ed.,

The Case for Biblical Christianity (Grand Rapids: Eerdmans, 1969), p. 36.

(51) Carnell, An Introduction to Christian Apologetics, p. 191n.

(52) Ibid., pp. 179, 192, 196.

(53) Carnell, The Theology of Reinhold Niebuhr, p. 119.

(54) Carnell, "Conservatives and Liberals Do Not Need Each Other," p. 36.

(55) Carnell, An Introduction to Christian Apologetics, p. 57. Carnell explains the law of contradiction in this way: "In any judgment a term must mean one thing at a time if it is to convey truth. The formal statement of the law of contradiction is as follows: A is not non-A." (p. 56-57). In this point also he sets himself against neo-orthodoxy's "existential tone." (See The Theology of Reinhold Niebuhr, p. 32).

(56) Carnell, A Philosophy of the Christian Religion, p. 41. On this point Joe E. Barnhart, "The Religious Epistemology and Theodicy of Edward John Carnell and Edgar Sheffield Brightman: A Study in Contrasts" (unpublished Ph.D. dissertation, Boston Univ., 1964), p. 119, writes "Carnell seems to mean that Scripture is not a criterion over against systematic consistency (including 'material fact') but rather is a special locus of systematic consistency within the broader whole of systematic consistency, for the Bible itself is considered by Carnell to be material information and evidence standing unified in perfect self-consistency."

(57) Ibid., pp. 40, 514.

(58) Edward John Carnell, The Kingdom of Love and the Pride of Life (Grand Rapids: Eerdmans, 1960), p. 118; Carnell, An Introduction to Christian Apologetics, p. 87.

(59) Carnell, A Philosophy of the Christian Religion, p. 29.

(60) Edward John Carnell, "Reinhold Niebuhr's View

of Scripture," Ronald H. Nash, ed., The Case for Biblical Christianity (Grand Rapids: Eerdmans, 1969), pp. 105, 109. "Immanence is the confidence that history contains its own meaning. Man needs only time and patience to acquire all significant truth. The Logos of history dwells within history" (p. 98).

(61) Carnell, The Case for Orthodox Theology, pp. 53, 54, 56.

(62) Ibid., pp. 59, 134. Carnell states this position clearly on p. 59: ". . . if the church teaches anything that offends the system of Romans and Galatians, it is cultic." Toward the end of the book (p. 134) he makes an even stronger statement: "A denomination is not part of the church if its creed or confession is out of harmony with the system of theology taught in Romans and Galatians."

(63) Ibid., pp. 55-56.

(64) William S. Sailer, "The Role of Reason in the Theologies of Nels Ferre and Edward J. Carnell" (unpublished S.T.D. dissertation, Temple Univ., 1964), p. 126.

(65) Carnell, The Theology of Reinhold Niebuhr, p. 57.

(66) Carnell, The Case for Orthodox Theology, p. 140.

(67) Ibid., p. 53. Each of these rules is explained in some detail on pp. 53-64.

(68) Edward John Carnell, "The Problem of Relisious Authority," His, Feb., 1950, p. 11.

(69) Carnell, The Case for Orthodox Theology, pp. 119-120.

(70) Carnell, An Introduction to Christian Apologetics, pp. 203, 201, 194.

(71) Carnell, "The Problem of Religious Authority," p. 12. Carnell supports his criticism of higher criticism with this statement: ". . . do I destroy the city of Paris when I presuppose on my world map that there is no place called Paris? No."

(72) Carnell, *An Introduction to Christian Apologetics*, pp. 193-194.

(73) Carnell, *The Theology of Reinhold Niebuhr*, p. 15.

(74) Carnell, *An Introduction to Christian Apologetics*, p. 193n.

(75) Carnell, *A Philosophy of the Christian Religion*, pp. 513-514. In this work Carnell sought to explain both the meaning and the short-comings of several value-options which vie for an individual's commitment. Now, at the end of the book, in an effort to explain the superior attractiveness and worth of orthodox Christianity, Carnell states that the individual may have, included in it, all the good of the other value-options. These options include pleasure, economic-social security, wisdom, and authority.

(76) Carnell, *An Introduction to Christian Apologetics*, p. 208; Carnell, *The Kingdom of Love and the Pride of Life*, p. 9.

(77) Carnell, *An Introduction to Christian Apologetics*, pp. 155-156.

(78) Carnell, "The Problem of Religious Authority," p. 11.

(79) Carnell, *The Case for Orthodox Theology*, p. 56.

(80) Jack T. Sanders, *Ethics in the New Testament* (Philadelphia: Fortress Press, 1975).

(81) James M. Gustafson, "The Place of Scripture in Christian Ethics: A Methodological Study," *Interpretation*, vol. 24.

(82) Carnell, *An Introduction to Christian Apologetics*, pp. 115-116.

(83) Ibid., p. 329. The verse is Gen. 9:6; "Whoever sheds the blood of man, by man shall his blood be shed; for God made man in his own image" (RSV).

(84) Edward John Carnell, "Should a Christian Go to War?" His, April, 1951, pp. 6-7.

(85) Ibid., p. 8.

(86) Edward John Carnell, "A Christian Social Ethics," The Christian Century, Aug. 7, 1963, pp. 979-980. Other examples of this use of Scripture in Carnell's writing may be found in Christian Commitment: An Apologetic, pp. 147-148, 214, 270; "Is Drunkenness a Sin?," United Evangelical Action, Mar. 1, 1948, p. 8; "The Christian and Television," His, May 1950, p. 1; "Should a Christian Go to War?," p. 8; "Capital Punishment and the Bible," Eternity, June 1961, p. 19.

(87) Carl F. H. Henry, Christian Personal Ethics (Grand Rapids: Baker, 1977); Carl F. H. Henry, Aspects of Christian Social Ethics (Grand Rapids: Eerdmans, 1964).

(88) Carnell, Christian Commitment: An Apologetic, pp. 207-208.

(89) Carnell, An Introduction to Christian Apologetics, p. 300.

(90) Carnell, "Is Drunkenness A Sin?," p. 6.

(91) Carnell, "Should A Christian Go to War?," p. 7. Other examples of this use of Scripture in Carnell's writing may be found in An Introduction to Christian Apologetics, p. 299; "Should A Christian Go to War?," p. 5; "Personal Happiness and Prosperity," Christan Economics, Sept. 3, 1957, p. 4.

(92) Carnell, "The Christian and Television," p. 2.

(93) Carnell, Christian Commitment: An Apologetic, p. 222. The verse is Matt. 26:41. Other examples of this use of Scripture occur on pp. 131 and 229.

(94) Carnell, "Is Drunkenness A Sin?," p. 6.

(95) Carnell, "Personal Happiness and Prosperity," p. 4.

(96) Ibid. Other instances where Christ is used as a model to be followed occur in Christian Commitment: An Apologetic, pp. 253-254 and "A Christian Social

Ethics," pp. 979-980.

(97) Carnell, *An Introduction to Christian Apologetics*, pp. 320-321. Carnell also used the example of Paul and the early church ("Personal Happiness and Prosperity," p. 4.), as well as Mary and Martha's reaction to the death of their brother with Jesus' resultant response (Edward John Carnell, "Evil--Why?," *Eternity*, Dec. 1960, pp. 22-24, 31.

(98) Andrew R. Osborn, *Christian Ethics* (London: Oxford Univ. Press, 1940).

(99) Carnell, "A Christian Social Ethics," pp. 979-980.

(100) Carnell, *Christian Commitment: An Apologetic*, pp. 164, 194; Edward John Carnell, "The Secret of Loving Your Neighbor," *Eternity*, July 1961, p. 16.

(101) Carnell, "The Christian and Television," p. 6. Other examples of this use of biblical principles can be found in *Christian Commitment: An Apologetic*, p. 152; "Personal Happiness and Prosperity," p. 4; "Evil--Why?," p. 24; and "The Bible and Capital Punishment," pp. 19-20.

(102) Carnell, *Christian Commitment: An Apologetic*, p. 92.

(103) Ibid., pp. 128-129.

(104) Ibid., pp. 230-231. Other examples of this use of Scripture occur in this book on pp. 25-26, 26, 27, 50-51, 97, 129, 138, 146-147, 170, 202, 208, 221, 222, 236, 239, and in *An Introduction to Christian Apologetics*, p. 282.

(105) Carnell, *The Kingdom of Love and the Pride of Life*, p. 5.

(106) Ibid., p. 6.

CHAPTER III

SELF-ACCEPTANCE AND MORAL KNOWLEDGE

Carnell began his major work in ethics by considering the problem encountered when a philosopher attempts to formulate a philosophy of life. His contention was that the source of knowledge which the philosopher neglects the most, and the one which is the most difficult to classify and isolate, is his or her own moral and spiritual environment. The philosopher has the option of ignoring this environment, yet the degree to which the environment is overlooked determines the degree to which the philosophy is inadequate to explain the whole of reality. Reality, it must be realized, is not something to be approached in relation to humanity, but in relation to distinct individuals. The real person is not the one who corresponds to the philosopher's "universal man." Rather, the only real person is one who suffers and fears and wrestles with the disparity between the actual moral self and the ideal moral self.(1)

Carnell argued that any thinking about Homo sapiens is but an abstraction. Such thinking does not refer to any particular person, but rather to abstractions of the race. To learn of the race is to learn data about a species. When the philosopher or scientist identifies this data with knowledge of a particular self, a major blunder is made, for the fact of the uniqueness of each individual prohibits identifying, at any point whatsoever, a person with the race.(2) "Only a perverted standard of values would induce others to neglect their individuality in favor of a scientific description of the race. To conprehend the species, but not the self, is sham scholarship."(3)

As a solution to the problem of neglect of the individual's moral and spiritual environment, Carnell proposed that any individual, not just the philosopher, can learn what it means to be held in such an environment merely by acquainting himself or herself with the realities to which he or she is committed by virtue of being an existing person. This acquainting process is a painful one, and cannot be done by proxy. It must be done by the individual, for only the individual knows the secrets of his or her moral and spiritual existence.(4) Carnell sounds like Kierkegaard at this point: ". . . the ethical, as being the internal, cannot be observed by an outsider. It can be realized only by the individual subject, who alone can know what it is that moves within him."(5)

Carnell's solution had its birth in his own experience as a philosopher. He readily admitted that even though he did not abuse philosophy, he was guilty of following a faulty philosophic method. Having committed himself to classical empiricism, he thought that feelings were the seeds of bad subjectivism.(6) After reading Kierkegaard, Carnell began to recognize the place of inwardness in philosophic method. Not long thereafter he changed his philosophic approach, asserting that "one rightly knows neither the self nor the universe until he spiritually comprehends himself in relation to the universe .... [T]he self is neither as simple in essense as I imagined, nor nearly as rationally subject to my control as I presumed."(7) Carnell's entire ethical theory was developed with this existential approach in mind. He felt, however, that existentialism was without a strong epistemological base, and thus set about the task of developing a method of knowing which would lead an individual into a knowledge of the realities to which he or she was committed by virtue of being an existing person.(8)

The Third Method of Knowing

Carnell approached his epistemological task in the existential realm by investigating the nature of truth, for without a clear understanding of the nature of truth, as commonly understood, he asserted, it would be impossible to develop an epistemology which would be adequate to lead an individual into a knowledge of the realities to which he or she was committed.

Philosophy typically acknowledges two kinds of truth. That which is real is true. "To the extent that something participates in being, it is true. This is called ontological truth.(9) It is "the sum total of reality itself."(10) Reality must be distinguished from appearance, however, and thus there must be a mental procedure which will put the human mind in contact with reality. Symbols and terms, representative of reality, need to be validly construed. This construal is done by means of the mental procedure of rational inference. When such inferences contain the real, they are true. This kind of truth is known as "propositional truth."

"<u>Propositional truth</u>, thus, is the second kind of truth."(11) This kind of truth "is systematic consistency or propositional correspondence to reality."(12) A proposition is true if it does not contradict our expectations when it is tested by not only the witness of the senses, but also our total conscious life, personal and social.

Corresponding to the two types of truth are two methods of knowing. Ontological truth is known by acquaintance, and propositional truth is known by inference. "<u>Knowledge by acquaintance</u> is the passage of the mind to a conclusion without the aid of a middle premise."(13) The condition which the subject must meet in order to gain knowledge by this method is direct experience, for only by direct experience can an individual apprehend what is.

> If one wants to know the sunset in all its presentational immediacy, he must face the west and open his eyes. He must experience the sunset...
> <u>Knowledge by inference</u> is the passage of the mind to a conclusion with the aid of a middle premise.(14)

Since syllogistic thinking is the basis of knowledge by inference, the rules of logic must always be followed when using this method of knowing. The condition of knowing which the subject must meet is the conceptual ordering of reality, the relating of thoughts in a consistent manner.

Carnell suggested, however, that the two methods of knowing are unable to acquaint the mind with a sense of duty. Some moralists, he charged, fallaciously try to gain a knowledge of duty by describing the differing ethical practices of humanity. This procedure, however, fails in its mission for two reasons. First, a description merely reviews existing practice; it cannot provide a sense of duty in the imperative mood. Second, a description is useless unless it can be proved that it is an expression of individuals carrying out what they inwardly believe, rather than what they want others to think they believe. Other moralists, Carnell observed, suppose that a knowledge of duty can be derived by an individual when he or she reviews his or her own feelings of duty. To think that such a knowledge will bring to the individual a sense of duty is erroneously to attempt to derive the imperative from the descriptive.(15) What Carnell had done, clearly, was to charge those who seek to gain a sense of duty from knowledge by acquaintance with committing the naturalistic fallacy.(16)

The greatest rational statement in morals, according to Carnell, was made by Immanuel Kant. Yet even Kant's work is impotent to bring the individual to a sense of duty, for "<u>Kantian ethics seeks to acquaint the mind with</u> duty by a rational statement of duty. Such an approach is doomed before it begins."(17) One can always ask why he or she should be rationally self-consistent. If he or she does not have a prior commitment to logic, then no logical argument concerning duty will be convincing. Knowledge by inference cannot bring to the individual a sense of duty. "Since people are free to decide whether or not they want to be rational, a formal statement of duty can confront the heart with nothing but <u>claims</u> to duty."(18) Carnell's basic criticism of the two methods of knowing is that they speak only of a person's descriptive essence. Another method of knowing must lead us into the imperative essence.

Before we can understand this third method of knowing, that method which Carnell asserted will lead the individual to a knowledge of the imperative essense, it is necessary to understand Carnell's view of the nature of truth, as well as his basic assumption regarding the development of a world view.

In keeping with his concept of God as the supreme authority for ethics, Carnell defined truth as "correspondence with the mind of God."(19) Any contact with truth is equivalent to contact with God, since God is truth.(20) Such a definition, however, will not clarify the third method of knowing, nor will it help us to see the third method in relation to the other two. Realizing this difficulty, Carnell expanded his definition of truth. Throughout his writings he insisted that truth is correspondence to things as they actually are. The real is the true.(21) He did not remain static in his thinking, however. At one point in his work in ethics he wrote "I feel strangely distant from the self that used to be." The primary change which he had in mind was his increasing awareness of the significance of the third method of knowing.(22) He realized he needed to augment his understanding of truth. Soon his definition became more inclusive. Objective reality was not eliminated from the definition, but at the same time objective reality no longer set the definition's limits.

> . . . [T]ruth is a correspondence between a thing and that which signifies it. Generally this correspondence is between a judgment and objective reality.. . . . But truth can also be predicated of a person. In this event the correspondence is between the total manner of his life, inward and outward, and the norm of rectitude. A true man is a good man.(23)

It was by introducing the subjective element into his view of truth that Carnell felt he could succeed in his epistemological task in the existential realm. The locus of the subjective element is the individual, for subjective truth, according to Carnell, "is concerned existence."(24) To understand better this element of Carnell's concept of truth, Kierkegaard, the one who inspired it, must be introduced.

Kierkegaard would not disagree with Carnell's early description of truth, for the former did not maintain that all truth is subjective, or that the only knowable truth is the subjective kind, but rather admitted that tautologies and analytic statements are true. He also agreed that objective truth is derived by means of reflection.(25) Yet he asserted that there is another kind of truth--subjective truth--which is revealed in the authentic ethical existence of the individual.

> It is therefore an existing spirit who is now conceived as raising the question of truth, presumably in order that he may exist in it; but in any case the question is raised by someone who is conscious of being a particular existing human being.(26)

It is this element of Kierkegaard's understanding of truth which led Carnell to augment his early definition of truth. Ultimately Carnell developed his ethical theory on the basis of Kierkegaard's concept of subjective truth. In developing his baffling assertion, "subjectivity is the truth,"(27) Kierkegaard wrote, "if the individual does not existentially and in existence lay hold of the truth, he will never lay hold of it."(28) By this he meant that truth is realized through personal appropriation. The subjective variety of truth is not an intellectual addition to the sum of objective truth in the individual's mind. Rather, it is the individual as he or she is transformed by ethical existence and decision. Out of repulsion to uncommitted confessional Christianity, Kierkegaard applied his concept of subjective truth to Christianity.

> Christianity protests every form of objectivity; it desires that the subject should be infinitely concerned about himself. It is subjectivity that Christianity is concerned with, and it is only in subjectivity that truth exists, if it exists at all; objectively, Christianity has absolutely no existence.(29)

Defining subjective truth, and opposing it to objectivity, Kierkegaard wrote,

> <u>An objective uncertainty held fast in an appropriation-process of the most passionate inwardness is the truth</u>, the highest truth attainable for an <u>existing individual</u>.. . . The paradoxical character of the truth is its objective uncertainty; this uncertainty is an expression for the passionate inwardness, and this passion is precisely the truth.(30)

Carnell adopted Kierkegaard's concept of subjective truth, at one point affirming as correct Kierkegaard's definition. Carnell understood Kierkegaard to mean, by his definition, "the subjective state of ethical decision, not that odious subjectivity which characterizes skepticism . . . [I]t is the being of becoming, the attaining of the existential assignment."(31) Having been convinced of the place of subjectivity in a world view, Carnell proposed a third kind of truth, parallel to the other two. "By the term 'third kind of truth,' I mean <u>truth as personal rectitude</u>."(32) Drawing upon his distinction between the descriptive essence and the imperative essence, he explained his definition in a way which equates rectitude with the comprehension of all human obligation: "Let us call the stuff of rectitude the 'imperative essence.' Even as the descriptive essence comprehends all that man is, so the imperative essence comprehends all that man ought to be."(33) This comprehension is not just intellectual, however. It is also volitional. "The possibility of rectitude is implied in the very meaning of moral freedom itself, for uprightness does not come into being until man as he is coincides with man as he ought to be."(34) What is it, though, that defines what man ought to be? Carnell asserted that this one fact answers that question: "<u>Man is not the author of his own existence.</u>"(35) Man is a dependent creature. The entire person must adjust himself or herself to this relationship of dependence.

> Dependence must be felt; it cannot be a mere object of thought . . . [A] person does not rightly apprehend dependence until he conforms himself to the relation. The necessity of this conformity is included in the relation itself. If an individual <u>professes</u> to be dependent, while he lives as if he were self-sufficient, he deceives himself and the truth is not in him.

Once the individual adjusts himself or herself to the fact of dependence, however, then the way is opened for the experience of the third kind of truth, the truth of understanding and being all that one should be. "Here, then, is the first clue to the third method of knowing: <u>Ultimate reality cannot be grasped unless rational knowledge is savored by spiritual conviction.</u>(36)

In developing a world view the philosopher must adjust his or her thinking to the fact that all people are dependent upon ultimate reality. Reality cannot be fully comprehended until one views it through the eyes of his or her own finitude. When dependence and finitude are included in a world view, and when the philosopher is transformed morally by the facts of dependence and finitude, then truth as personal rectitude comes into being in the life of the philosopher. The moral freedom to make decisions has been properly exercised and the responsibility of creating rectitude has been accepted. Knowledge in the moral sphere can now be gained through the third method of knowing.

Carnell defined knowledge as "man's systematic contact with the real."(37) The issue before us now is how an individual may systematically contact reality in the moral sphere. Carnell asserted that a person can have knowledge of the imperative essence's content only if he or she spiritually accepts (that is, volitionally submits to) the truth to which he or she is committed by virtue of the fact of being an existing individual in this world. Intellectual assent to the truth is insufficient to lead to the imperative essence. The individual must allow personal transformation to take place in light of the truth. That truth primarily is the fact that all people are dependent and finite. The choice to allow such transformation to take place is a praiseworthy one, for moral choice forms the essence of personal dignity. If a person will not make this choice willfully, then nothing can compel the individual. The fact of dependence and finitude forms the essence of the moral and spiritual environment in which the individual lives. If he or she will not submit to the fact of dependence and finitude, preferring rather to deal with rational or empirical claims to duty, then a knowledge of the imperative essence can never be personally felt.(38)

Carnell is once again sounding like Kierkegaard. Describing what Carnell called "knowledge of the imperative essence" as "the good of eternal happiness," Kierkegaard wrote,

> Christianity proposes to endow the individual with an eternal happiness, a good which is not distributed wholesale, but only to one individual at a time. Though Christianity assumes that there inheres in the subjectivity of the individual, as being the potentiality of the appropriation of this good, the possibility for its acceptance, it does not assume that the subjectivity is immediately ready for such acceptance or even that it has, without further ado, a real conception of the significance of such a good. The development or transformation of the individual's subjectivity, its infinite concentration

> in itself . . . this constitutes the
> developed potentiality of the primary
> potentiality which subjectivity as such
> presents.(39)

Moral knowledge cannot be gained except by volitional concentration upon the self. According to Kierkegaard,

> For a subjective reflection the truth becomes
> a matter of appropriation, of inwardness, of
> subjectivity, and thought must probe more and
> more deeply into the subject and his
> subjectivity.. . . It is a misunderstanding
> to be concerned about reality from the
> aesthetic or intellectual point of view.. . .
> [T]he only question of reality that is
> ethically pertinent, is the question of one's
> own reality.(40)

Carnell was not merely echoing Kierkegaard as he developed the third method of knowing. Rather, he was consciously borrowing Kierkegaardian thought and reworking it into an ethical epistemology. In posing the possibility of the existence of a third method of knowing and a third kind of truth, he used Kierkegaard's words, "comes into being," to characterize the kind of truth which is produced as one is transformed by ethical decision. Further, he acknowledged the concept as Kierkegaardian.(41) Carnell just changed Kierkegaard's language to fulfill his epistemological task.

The Dane's concept of the "good of eternal happiness" was restated by Carnell as "knowledge of the imperative essence." His concept of "subjectivity of the individual" became "the power of moral choice;" "personal reality" became "the truth to which one is committed by virtue of existence." Paralleling the two conventional methods of knowing, while maintaining a distinction from them, Carnell identified his third method of knowing.

> I shall call the third method of knowing
> __knowledge by moral self-acceptance__. The
> content of the imperative essence cannot
> be apprehended until one is spiritually
> transformed by the sum of those duties
> which already hold him.(42)

Explaining further what knowledge by moral self-acceptance means, Carnell showed how it differs from experiential or conceptual knowledge. One may be experientially or conceptually unaware of the implications of his or her actions, and thus may be viewed as ignorant. He or she has not come into contact with and submitted to the realities of his or her moral and spiritual environment. If, however, the individual is rationally conscious of the truth to which he or she is committed by virtue of existing, and can anticipate the implications of freely-chosen moral actions, then that person can be viewed as having knowledge, for he or she is responsible for knowing the results of actions.(43) At this point the third condition of knowing emerges.

The condition of knowing which corresponds to knowledge by acquaintance is direct experience, and the condition which corresponds to knowledge by inference is the conceptual ordering of reality. Yet "what condition of knowing," Carnell asked, "answers to moral self-acceptance?" Since moral freedom composes human dignity, "whenever the consequences of a choice can be anticipated, a decision to act implies the responsibility to live by these consequences."(44) If a person acts imprudently, our response is, "You know better than that!" for imprudence is an offense to knowledge. This concept is Carnell's third condition of knowing.

> To say that an individual "knows" better is merely another way of saying that he is responsible for acquainting himself with the outcome of his choices. And this is precisely what is meant by the third condition of knowing: <u>To know is to be morally responsible for knowing</u>.(45)

There is a uniqueness to the third condition of knowing as over against the other two conditions. Every person automatically meets the third condition if he or she is a normal human being, for we are born with the duty to be responsible in the moral choices we make. If a person neglects this duty, then he or she can never gain knowledge in the imperative realm, knowledge by moral self-acceptance.(46) Kierkegaard expressed the same need for the individual to accept the duty to be responsible with regard to himself or herself and the choices which he or she makes. There is a relationship between the self, the need to choose, and duty.

> [A person] does not become another man than he was before, but he becomes himself, consciousness is unified, and he is himself.. . . Ethically the ideality is the real within the individual himself. The real is an inwardness that is infinitely interested in existing; this is exemplified in the ethical individual.(47)

In Carnellian language, the unified conscience and the inwardness that is interested in existing are known as knowledge by moral self-acceptance.

Anticipating that someone, in response to his third condition of knowing, would ask, "How much does an individual know?," Carnell wrote, "He knows as much as he may be held accountable for." The extent of a person's knowledge by moral self-acceptance may be "measured by the power of moral and rational self-transcendence to acquaint the mind with consequences that flow from freely motivated conduct."(48) When the outcome of a particular action cannot be anticipated, then knowledge by moral self-acceptance is inoperative.

From his development of the third method of knowing, Carnell concluded that if a person will be spiritually honest, submitting to the realities to which he or she is committed by virtue of the fact that he or she is an existing person, then he or she will realize that he or she has the basic outline of a world view which incorporates the whole of reality, including the existence of God. "It is my conviction that man's difficulty is not lack of knowledge, but lack of moral courage to act on the knowledge he already has."(49)

The rest of Carnell's thought regarding moral self-acceptance is built upon the foundation of the third method of knowing. Kierkegaardian thought was basic to Carnell, for it provided Carnell with the conceptual framework which he designated "the loci of truth."(50) Carnell was impressed with Kierkegaard for three reasons. First, Kierkegaard used the Bible in a way which struck Carnell as proper for the development of Christian ethics. For this reason Kierkegaard secured a firm place in Carnell's mind, for the Bible and the Bible alone was Carnell's epistemic moral authority. Writing of Kierkegaard Carnell stated,

> Even though (to our knowledge) he never bothered to develop convincing rules of hermeneutics, he nonetheless had such a sense of biblical propriety that he was able to level a successful charge against the ethical standards of both the local Lutheran fellowship and the church at large. He was convinced--and rightly so--that far too many ethicists were quagmired in legalism.(51)

Second, Kierkegaard impressed Carnell not as the heretic which so many conservatives accused him of being, but as one of God's faithful servants. In Carnell's mind Kierkegaard received from God not condemnation or punishment, but an eternal reward.(52) Third, the scholar in Carnell apparently was awed at the intellectual prowess which Kierkegaard demonstrated in the ethical sphere. Again speaking of Kierkegaard, Carnell wrote, "In my opinion his power as an ethicist peers that of Socrates, Plato, or Augustine. The Christian community has yet to penetrate the profundity of his book <u>Works of Love</u>."(53)

Kierkegaard was everything that Carnell could hope for in a model. He used the Bible properly, he displayed spiritual maturity, and he had an intellect which rivaled any that could be named. Carnell thus was pleased to acknowledge openly that Kierkegaard was his mentor.

> I must say, it is easy to follow the very one who wanted no followers. Without the stimulation of the Danish gadfly, I probably never would have learned how to ask questions from the perspective of inwardness. It is a pleasure to acknowledge my indebtedness to Kierkegaard.(54)

Carnell took more than just Kierkegaard's methodology of asking questions, however. He went on to assert that he and Kierkegaard were doing the same thing. "I felt somewhat like a wayfarer who, having come a long distance by himself, is suddenly joined by one going to the same country."(55) He found guidance, at least in part, in Kierkegaard.(56)

Kierkegaard is generally acknowledged as the father of modern existentialism. For Carnell he was "the focal point of reference for all future existentialism."(57) Now what Kierkegaard was attempting to do was to show that Christianity should be viewed as a living truth demanding the passionate involvement of the individual who was in the state of becoming. What he observed in his native Copenhagen, however, was impassionate professing Christians whose faith had been reduced to the affirmation of a doctrinal system and the recitation of the proper creed. In his own time and place Carnell observed that a similar expression of Christianity dominated Protestant fundamentalism. A person was viewed as orthodox not if he or she demonstrated a passionate living faith, but if he or she ascribed to the five fundamentals and denounced modernism. His attempt in developing the third method of knowing and the notion of moral self-acceptance was to emulate Kierkegaard. It is no wonder, then, that he affirms Kierkegaard as an apologist of the third kind of truth.(58)

Carnell saw that Kierkegaard, in developing an existential approach to the individual, was doing several things which he wanted to imitate. First, Kierkegaard was attempting to bring the individual and God closer together. The goal in mind was personal spiritual vitality. By giving a fresh interpretation to spiritual truth the body of Christ was enriched.(59) Second, Kierkegaard was appealing to people to rediscover the value of moral action. "With extraordinary insight he perceived that the ethical exists only when the individual mediates the terms of ethical decision in his own volitional life. Apart from the act the ethical is nonexistent."(60) By observing how one acts, another can observe the ethical and comprehend the meaning of the law of life. Third, Kierkegaard was stressing the fact that individuality consists in passionate, ethical decision. When a person flees moral decision by submitting to objective security, such as the church or a priestly class, he or she relinquishes individuality.(61) Carnell attempted to speak Kierkegaard's message to Protestant orthodoxy in the United States. His goal was to foster spiritual vitality by motivating individuals to become passionate about their faith, not passionate against modernists.

The road to such a redirection of passion he determined was first trod by Kierkegaard, and was defined by Kierkegaard's three imitable efforts. By the end of his work in ethics Carnell was not defending his use of Kierkegaard, but rather employing him without apology as backing for his thought.(62)

In <u>A Philosophy of the Christian Religion</u> he credited Kierkegaard with providing a convincing defense of the third kind of truth, making explicit what Christianity had always assumed.(63) It was out of a desire to follow Kierkegaard, and even to go beyond him, that Carnell developed his theory of knowledge by moral self-acceptance. We have already noted that he thought that existentialism lacked a sufficient epistemological foundation,(64) and that his work would provide the necessary foundation. He also attempted to develop a methodology by which an individual can become acquainted with the moral sphere, one which paralleled the scientific method and the philosophic method. As was the case with his epistemological foundation, he felt the methodology he developed was an original contribution to moral thought.(65) Carnell may have been inconsistent when distinguishing ethical methodology from those of philosophy and science, for at one point, in criticizing Kierkegaard, Carnell supported "ethics as a science."(66) If ethics is a science, then how can ethical methodology be something other than scientific methodology? Carnell neglected to answer this question.

The framework of Carnell's work was introspective self-questioning, for which Kierkegaard served as a model. In a <u>Journal</u> entry Kierkegaard wrote of his "maieutic carefulness" and his "proceeding slowly and continually letting it seem as if I knew nothing more."(67) Each question, when answered, led to another question which pried deeper into the moral commitments of the individual. This search of the soul appears on the surface to be quite existential, particularly a Kierkegaardian brand of existentialism. To provide an existential ethical epistemology and methodology in the Kierkegaardian tradition which was palatable to evangelicals was Carnell's goal. Yet on a number of major questions he appears to be anything but Kierkegaardian. At some points he was even strongly critical of Kierkegaard.

Kierkegaard's attempt was to release people from their imprisonment to illusion, a state of total misconception of the truth, and to change their entire self-understanding and world view. For him the worst illusion was the one in which individuals approach life as observers rather than participants, an illusion known as objectivity. The task of philosophy, for Kierkegaard, was to transfer people from the darkness of objective illusion to the light of subjective truth. That transfer, of necessity, requires the obliteration of the distinction between the rational and the volitional, for subjective truth cannot be only an object of intellectual assent. It must also involve the will of the individual who submits to its claims. In the moral realm, then, the subjective person cannot separate epistemology from ethics. Knowledge cannot be divorced from action.

For Kierkegaard the one major concern of any person should rest in the quest to be subjective truth. The individual must turn from all systems and general truth, and must, through introspection, seek to discover his or her own personal truth and means to personal fulfillment. The ethical goal of each individual is one that only he or she can realize existentially. The task of becoming subjective is a personal and individual struggle, one for which there can be no substitute.

> The highest degree of resignation that a human being can reach is to acknowledge the given independence in every man, and after the measure of his ability do all that can in truth be done to help someone preserve it.(68)

Each person must find the truth for himself or herself. He or she cannot be told the truth, for "only the truth which edifies is truth for you."(69)

Kierkegaard followed Socrates in believing that subjective truth cannot be communicated as objective content through propositions, but only by means of a maieutic art. Even the communication of truth through the symbol of words is objective and must be rejected. What then of philosophic systems of truth? They must be rejected also as a means to the achievement on the part of the individual of subjectivity. Philosophic systems concern the intellect only, whereas subjectivity requires the participation of the whole person.

> Nothing must then be incorporated in a logical system that has any relation to existence, that is not indifferent to existence. The infinite preponderance which the logical as the objective has over all thinking is again limited by the fact that seen subjectively it is an hypothesis, precisely because it is indifferent to existence in the sense of actuality.(70)

Such a logical system which claims to be the truth cannot be tested by thinking. Rather, it can be tested only by the existing individual.

Truth which cannot be communicated objectively and directly, for Kierkegaard, can be known only as each person, in becoming subjective, turns from logic to the paradoxical and absurd. This turn is equally difficult for the stupid as well as the wise.

> Every man, the wisest and the simplest, can qualitatively . . . distinguish just as essentially between what he understands and what he does not understand, and he can discover that there is something which is, in spite of the fact that it is against his understanding and way of thinking.(71)

In order to become subjective, the individual must confront the paradox of existence, the absurd, and must affirm it, while denying the law of contradiction held to by the proponents of systems of philosophy and science. Criticizing Kant in this regard, Kierkegaard wrote:

> For it is the duty of the human understanding to understand that there are things which it cannot understand, and what these are. Human understanding has vulgarly occupied itself with nothing but understanding, but if it would only take the trouble to understand itself at the same time it would simply have to posit the paradox.

> The paradox is not a concession but a category, an ontological definition which expresses the relation between an existing cognitive spirit and eternal truth.(72)

The logician must reconcile contradictory statements. They have no place in his or her system. The subjective individual must affirm them, however, for, to Kierkegaard, life is nothing if it is not a contradition.

The subjective person demonstrates his or her affirmation of the paradoxical, the contradictory, and the absurd by the exercise of faith. Faith, along with these other three concepts, is an existential category, inherent in the definition of subjectivity. Faith is not a result of scientific investigation and accumulation of data, but "is the highest passion in the sphere of human subjectivity."(73) Passion cannot be a scientific category, and thus may not be investigated by the scientific method. A scientific approach to faith seeks to make faith a matter of certainty resulting from empirical data. Kierkegaard, however, held that "if passion is eliminated, faith no longer exists, and certainty and passion do not go together."(74) If passion is a precondition to faith, then the leap is its expression. The leap of faith necessitates a risk, "for without risk there is no faith, and the greater the risk the greater the faith; the more objective security the less inwardness, . . . and the less objective security the more profound the possible inwardness."(75) Regarding his own faith, he wrote of objective uncertainty.(76) Christianity was not a confessional orthodoxy to Kierkegaard, but "an existential communication expressing an existential contradiction."(77)

Some of the areas in which Carnell is not Kierkegaardian have been enumerated and explained well by others.(78) There is only one major difference between the two men, but it found expression in several subjects. Those subjects are systematization, verification, faith, and subjectivity versus objectivity. All expressions of the difference actually were examples of the one disagreement: the place of reason in commitment. Continuing his picture of two people on a journey together, Carnell wrote,

> . . . when they unexpectedly confront a fork in the road, each adamantly defies the judgment of the other. In the end they must go their separate ways, for each tenaciously clings to his own convictions. Though keenly regretting the loss of fellowship, each must courageously venture the hope that wisdom is on his side.(79)

In Carnell's mind Kierkegaard's error was that he over-reacted to dead orthodoxy(80) in "setting the rational self against the moral self."(81) According to Carnell, Kierkegaard mistakenly thought that the use of reason tended to retard the development of moral commitment.

Carnell took it upon himself to offer what he felt was a correction of the Kierkegaardian mistake. He accurately pointed out that Kierkegaard was not totally against reason, but merely tried to restrict the domain in which reason was authoritative. In Carnell's thinking, however, this attempt by Kierkegaard was tantamount to an abandonment of reason.(82) He did, however, credit Kierkegaard with the highest of motives.

> Kierkegaard concluded that the best way to preserve both Christianity and individuality is to set the subjective witness in opposition to the objective, proportioning the certainty of the former to the uncertainty of the latter.
>
> It is very easy for one to sympathize with Kierkegaard's intentions. . .
>
> But it is not easy for one to sympathize with the method Kierkegaard elected in preserving Christianity. A <u>healthy</u> inwardness must be guided by, and proportional to, objective evidence.(83)

Reason and evidences were absolutely necessary in Carnell's conception of inwardness. When Kierkegaard abandoned reason, Carnell refused to accept further guidance from him.(84) Carnell grounded his refusal in his anthropology.

> Being a rational creature, thus, man must proportion his spiritual commitments to what the mind can consciously clear.. . .
>
> Therefore Kierkegaard's advice that we believe against the understanding cannot commend itself to a person who still respects the fact that he is made in the image of God. Rationality is so integral to our nature that when we betray it in favor of a higher understanding, we corrupt our own person.(85)

Sealing his break from Kierkegaard over the place of reason Carnell concluded,

> [H]owever harmless Kierkegaard's theory of inwardness may have first appeared, the perspective of time proves that it contains the sting of death in it. Whoever takes up the sword of setting the heart against the head will perish by that sword.(86)

The reason Carnell so strongly opposed Kierkegaard on the issue of the place of reason in inwardness is found in his concept of authority. The undeniable epistemic moral authority for Carnell was the Bible, and on the issue of the use of reason he concluded that Kierkegaard was unbiblical. Previously Carnell had chosen Kierkegaard as a model because of his sense of biblical propriety. Yet when Carnell sensed an area where Kierkegaard, according to Carnell, was unbiblical, compromise was rejected. The authority of the Bible was absolute to Carnell. All other authorities had to submit to the absolute authority.

> Submission to the system of Biblical Christianity is good, not because complacency is destroyed by absurdities, but because the system is able to support spirituality through its rigorous systematic consistency. If a man seeks to increase inwardness, therefore, let him <u>adorn</u>, not belittle, that metaphysical <u>system</u> which alone makes being an individual--or anything

else--meaningful.(87)

An example of the way Kierkegaard and Carnell clashed can be seen in the issue of faith. For Kierkegaard reason was a hindrance to faith, for faith comes through a commitment to the absurd and paradoxical.(88) "Faith begins precisely where thinking leaves off."(89) Carnell, however, attacked Kierkegaard on this point.(90) For Carnell, reason is the guardian of the third kind of truth, "for apart from its council the heart would never fully recognize when the conditions of inward truth have been met." Since we are rational, we must commit ourselves only to those things which clear the exercise of our minds,(91) for "whatever else faith may be, it is at least a 'resting of the mind in the sufficiency of evidences.' The extent of this sufficiency is measured by a cool and dispassionate use of reason."(92) For Carnell, then, "a faith based on rational evidences is able to nourish a healthy inwardness."(93) If our conduct in life is able to suggest any axiom, it is the following:

> The native person--the one unaffected by corrupting philosophic presuppositions--is at his best, and is most ideally a man of faith, when he obeys, rather than defies, the report of a critically developed understanding.(94)

The concepts of the leap of faith and the need for objective uncertainty were central to Kierkegaard's understanding. Yet, as may be expected, Carnell rejected them also. He wrote, "There is no 'leap' in faith. While faith may involve a cordial commitment of the whole man to Jesus Christ, it is a passion which is drawn out by objectively measurable evidence."(95) While asserting that in some instances knowledge by inference must defer to knowledge by acquaintance, he was quick to stop short of Kierkegaard. "But such an admission in no way supports the assumption that evangelical confrontation is a passionate leap in the face of objective paradox."(96) Carnell's whole underlying concept of the authority of the Bible surfaces on the question of the leap of faith.

> In no instance do the Scriptures encourage the penitent to believe that by a subjective "leap" of faith he may

> atone for a deficiency in objective
> authority. On the contrary, cordial
> trust is always grounded in reasonable
> evidences.(97)

He defended his statement by citing the instance of the apostle Thomas after the resurrection, in which the level of faith was directly, not inversely, proportional to the sufficiency of the evidences. In his criticism of Kierkegaard's concept of certainty, Carnell made a similar observation.

> Kierkegaard said that certainty and
> passion do not go together. This is not
> a very convincing philosophic position
> to take, for certainty comes into being
> whenever the evidences are deemed
> sufficient.. . . As far as the state of
> certainty is concerned, <u>the one and only
> issue is the sufficiency of the
> evidences</u>. All else is beside the
> point. This means that apart from a
> state of certainty, we have no right to
> claim that we are in possession of
> truth.(98)

At the outset of this chapter it was pointed out that Carnell's teaching regarding the error of the philosopher and scientist was that both neglected the individual in their quest to describe the abstraction, "humanity." They made a major blunder, he argued, when they sought to apply data about the race to any particular person, for each person's uniqueness prohibits identification of that person, at any point, with the race. Any attempt so to identify an individual is sham scholarship. Carnell's critique was Kierkegaardian. In the <u>Concluding Unscientific Postscript</u> Kierkegaard wrote,

> Being an individual man is a thing that
> has been abolished, and every
> speculative philosopher confuses himself
> with humanity at large, whereby he
> becomes something infinitely great--and
> at the same time nothing at all. He
> confounds himself with humanity in sheer
> distraction of mind.. . . And when one
> finds that every basement-dweller can
> play the game of being humanity, one

> learns at last that being purely and
> simply a human being is a more
> significant thing than playing the
> society game in this fashion. And one
> thing more. When a basement-dweller
> plays this game everyone thinks it
> ridiculous; and yet it is equally
> ridiculous for the greatest man in the
> world to do it.(99)

In developing his third method of knowing, however, Carnell ironically committed the very act which he denounced in philosophers and scientists, for his third method of knowing is applicable only to an ideal type, the "universal person." He neglected the uniqueness of each individual, proposing instead a method by which any alert and willing person can arrive at given conclusions regarding the moral and spiritual environment.(100) This method, or any other which aims at the recognition on the part of the user of universal moral laws certainly is not Kierkegaardian, for Kierkegaard's ethics emphasized striving, not duty toward moral laws.

Carnell began his ethics by stating what he considered to be an absolute truth, that "<u>man is not the author of his own existence</u>."(101) This truth he felt did not need to be demonstrated, but merely emphasized. On this truth of human dependence he built the rest of his ethics. Yet the statement of an absolute truth for everyone, in the subjective realm, is not of Kierkegaard, for he regarded truth as something which was valid ony if it was truth for the subjective person.

In <u>Christian Commitment: An Apologetic</u>, Carnell appears to have disclosed his own spiritual odyssey. Such a disclosure would be existential if Carnell had not shifted from self-disclosure to prescription. The self-disclosure is existential, but the prescription is based uppon rationality, logic, and empiricism. Carnell used his own life as the data, and built for himself an interpretive framework on which to hang the data. He assumed that any person who would conduct the same experiment would arrive at the same data. This assumption is the point at which he disregarded the uniqueness of each person, relying rather on his notion of the "universal person." He should have realized, as do most existentialists, that not all people seeking to gain knowledge in the moral realm will arrive at the same experiential data. In addition to his assumption about data, however, his prescription regarding his interpretive framework (i.e., that his interpretive framework should be the one adopted by every person who is sensitive to the moral realm) made him anything but an existentialist.

The Application of the Third Method of Knowing

Moral self-acceptance does not stop with the individual. Carnell expanded the idea to include not only the individual's relationship with himself or herself, but also relationships between people. His attempt was to apply the third condition of knowing to the social sphere. In the personal sphere he had asked, "To what realities am I committed by virtue of being an existing person?" That question in the social sphere is converted to, "To what realities am I committed when I freely stand in the society of others?" Upon reflection Carnell realized that he, and everyone else, was committed to what he termed the law of dignity: "<u>Once we enter society with an eye to the third condition of knowing, we find that we are powerless to trust others unless they give evidence of accepting the dignity of our person</u>.. . . The sheer presence of our person places others under moral responsibility."(102) When a person enters our presence, we instantly and automatically demand that he or she give evidence of accepting the moral responsibility of regarding our dignity by means of a handshake or other friendly gesture. If he or she is not willing to accept such responsibility, then he or she never should have entered the circle of nearness. Knowledge of the imperative essence was contingent upon accepting the realities to which we are committed by virtue of existing, and interpersonal exchange which results from fellowship is contingent upon both parties accepting the law of dignity.

The law of dignity usually is not either totally accepted or totally rejected. Rather, it is accepted in degrees, depending upon the level of intimacy of the relationship. "Friends must give stronger evidences than strangers; kin must give more intimate evidence than friends.. . . We will trust a stranger only to the degree that he shows a want of conscious intention to harm us."(103) When two people enter into fellowship, neither is at liberty to ask if the other wishes to be

treated as a human being, with dignity. Even moral
neutrality with respect to a person's dignity is
impossible if fellowship is to remain, for fellowship
itself requires that both parties accept the realities
to which they are committed when entering into society,
that is, the law of dignity. The third kind of truth,
truth as personal rectitude, is contingent upon the
acceptance of this law. "Truth as personal rectitude
comes into being, or goes out of being, in direct
proportion to an individual's willingness to be
inwardly transformed by the requirements of rectitude.
The imperative essence does not exist until one is
moral."(104)

    A difficulty is encountered when the reality of
the law of dignity is affirmed. When one person enters
the circle of nearness of another, the latter, since he
or she is committed to the law of dignity, demands that
the former offer some evidence of respect for his or
her dignity. Simultaneously, however, the latter will
be repulsed by any act which appears to be promted by
duty rather than sincere desire. It seems, then, that
the latter, by virtue of his or her commitment to the
law of dignity, makes a demand upon the former which
cannot be met. The act must be both necessary and
free. Yet how can these two opposites be reconciled?

    Carnell asserted that there is only one means of
reconciliation.

> <u>Morality consists in choices that are
> freely expressed through the necessities
> of the moral and spiritual environment.</u>
> A moral act is free because it is
> natural; and it is necessary because it
> flows from the moral and spiritual
> environment. Morality is a fruit, not a
> work. It cannot be aroused by rational
> or volitional striving . . . freedom and
> necessity can be combined in no other
> manner.

Freedom expressed through necessity is the paradox of
morals. When a person submits to the claims of the
moral and spiritual environment, acts of respect for
others' dignity become spontaneous for the person has
been transformed, and they become necessary for the
moral and spiritual environment can produce nothing
else.

> As we submit to the moral and spiritual environment, God graciously meets our humility by creating right affections in us; and these right affections, in turn, excite a spontaneous desire to be upright. The less conflict there is between duty and desire, the more perfect our actions become.

On the other hand, when a person's motivation for right action is desire to conform through human striving to the requirements of law, that person's actions are void of value, for law is more highly honored than dignity. Unconscious spontaneity has vanished. We are offended by the person's affected effort, for "the supposition is that if it were not for law, one would be morally free to decide whether or not it is to his wider advantage to respect us."(105) The law of dignity has been spurned.

It must be emphasized that a person must enter our circle of nearness if our moral sense is to be aroused. Unknown people, though dying of starvation, will not affect our moral sentiment if they are so distant that they appear to be mere statistics. What do we experience, however, when someone enters our circle of nearness? The third method of knowing teaches us that no matter who the person may be, if we allow that person to reveal the intimacies of his or her heart, there is automatically aroused in us a sense of moral obligation toward that person. We are obligated to respect his or her dignity, since this obligation is a reality to which we are committed when entering fellowship.(106)

Carnell continued his inquiry into moral self-acceptance and social relations by considering what happens when those who enter our presence disregard our dignity.

> Since I had previously asked, "To what moral realities am I committed when others enter the circle of nearness?" I now decided it would be in accord with good procedure if I simply extended the question and asked, "To what moral realities am I committed when those in the circle of nearness refuse to show

signs of fellowship?"

His initial response was,

> <u>Whenever others offend my dignity, I
> judge them guilty</u>. Judgment flows with
> instantaneous spontaneity; I simply
> cannot look with moral indifference on
> acts of inconsideration.(107)

We are powerless to overcome our involuntary response of judging others. We demand that others regard our dignity. When they do not, we judge them guilty and withhold fellowship from them.

Carnell realized that his response to his own question, if it were to be credible, would have to overcome the possible charge that the automatic judging of those who offend the law of dignity does not reflect the moral and spiritual environment in which we all live, but rather is merely an expression of personal disgruntlement and preoccupation with self. Being determined to overcome the charge, he started by clarifying the term, "personal dignity." That clarification did not come in the form of a definition. Carnell felt that dignity is something which can be known only as it is felt. Knowledge by acquaintance is the means by which we come to know the essence of dignity. Yet personal dignity is not completely unavailable to the detached observer, for dignity does have social manifestations. It is at this point that Carnell attempted to answer the hypothetical critic, asserting that to judge others as guilty is to state that inherent human rights have been violated, rather than to express personal disgruntlement and preoccupation with self.

> Dignity expresses itself in the form of
> human rights. That is why one is
> justified in speaking of either dignity
> or rights. Even as dignity comprehends
> the secret essence of personality, so
> rights comprehend its social expression.
> Dignity is a name for our spiritual
> essence, while rights are the field on
> which this essence stretches its limbs.

When pressed as to the content of human rights, Carnell answered, "Life, liberty, and the pursuit of happiness are the stuff of human rights." Since he had equated dignity and rights, he was free to restate his question in a form which could more readily be approached. The question now became, "To what moral realities are we committed when our rights are violated?"(108) Before answering the question, however, Carnell needed to digress.

Carnell realized that feelings of indignation are aroused not only by unjust treatment at the hands of others, but also by personal repulsion and offended individual taste. The actions of an uncourteous clerk in a nursery arouse the same feelings as the fetid odor given off by the mound of fresh fertilizer at the rear of the store. How can the indignant feelings which are morally defensible be separated from those which are not? Since judicial feelings are aroused by situations other than those in which our personal dignity has been violated, we must devise a means for distinguishing the violated-rights situations from the others.(109)

Carnell held that this notion was the clue to distinguishing morally-defensible situations from others:

> A <u>morally provoked feeling can be defended with the consent of our nobler faculties and the praise of men of character</u>. A defense of justice edifies the soul, while a defense of peevishness deteriorates it.

Character is simply moral steadiness, the prime attribute of those who have submitted to the claims of the moral and spiritual environment. Morally-defensible instances of judicial feelings, then, are those in which all upright people (those who have submitted to the claims of the moral and spiritual environment) would make a judgment of guilt without feeling spiritually insecure. They would all leave the situation feeling morally clean.(110) The impossibility of achieving a unanimous judgment is an issue which Carnell neglected to treat. Yet, presuming Carnell's solution to the problem of distinguishing those situations in which a guilty verdict can be defended from those in which it cannot, the central question can now be answered.

Carnell's initial response to the question was

that he judged offenders guilty. Upon reflection, however, he altered his response. "We are committed to the assurance that those who do this are guilty, for we can defend our sense of indignation with the consent of our nobler faculties and the praise of men of character." To cease judging offenders is parallel to ceasing to feel a sense of personal dignity, for "charging inconsiderate individuals with guilt is merely the reverse side of our demand that our dignity be respected." We cannot cease either action, for our commitment is to a moral absolute. "A spiritual defense of our dignity, and the judicial condemnation of those who violate it, are complementary claims of the one moral and spiritual environment. We cannot block the flow of these claims without atrophying character."(111) The offended moral faculty is known as the judicial sentiment.

The individual who accepts Carnell's answer to the question immediately encounters a difficulty. The fact of our participation in the moral and spiritual environment authorizes us to demand respect for our dignity and to judge as guilty those who arouse our judicial sentiment, yet it dos not authorize us to carry out the penalty of the law. We simultaneously cannot ignore violations of our persons and cannot seek revenge, since we are only the law's custodians, not its enforcers. To show that this is true, an individual need only monitor his or her own feelings when he or she attempts to administer justice. The feelings will be much like those produced when a person attempts to give moral justification for an indignant response to a situation which offends personal taste but not personal dignity. The nobler faculties are disgraced and the moral life deteriorates. Any attempt to dispense justice merely reveals one's sense of revenge. Personal shame is the result.(112)

We cannot enforce the law because we live and move and have our being in God. The moral and spiritual environment in which we all participate from the first moment of moral self-consciousness is the omnipresent God. We bear, in our persons, the divine image, in that we share God's commitment to the law of justice.

> An aroused judicial sentiment is merely heaven's warning that the image of God is being outraged.. . . Our participation in God issues in a

> spiritual intuition of our own dignity, on the one hand, and the guilt of those who violate it on the other.

Just as God never lets us lose a sense of personal dignity, so he makes it impossible for us to overlook inconsiderate acts on the part of others. The guilty must give an account before an administrator of justice, or the outraged judicial sentiment will never be placated.(113) If it be objected that there need not be an administrator of justice, then Carnell's response is that the objector should review the realities to which he or she is committed and make a choice between the alternatives posed by that commitment.

> Since guilt means "liability for the transgression of the law," it would of necessity follow that if unjust and inconsiderate people were not answerable to a lawful tribunal we could never with moral propriety judge them.. . . [U]nless the moral and spiritual environment authorizes us to be custodians of the law we could not meaningfully say that those who disregard us are culpable. So we are confronted with a forced option. Either we must once for all desist from the habit of judging those who mistreat us, or we must spiritually adjust ourselves to the reality--<u>not just the possibility</u>--of the administrator of justice.

Since nobody can deny the existence of the administrator without contradicting himself or herself through a disowning of his or her own instinctive commitment to the guilt of those who offend personal dignity, the administrator's reality is established.(114)

The one issue which remains is to clarify the nature of the administrator of justice. At the outset of his response to the question of to what or to whom are guilty individuals responsible, Carnell made the point that they must answer to a person, not a thing, for only a person is free to hear and judge evidence. He defined person as "<u>freedom expressed through moral</u>

self-consciousness," and concluded that the administrator of justice and the ground of our being (moral and spiritual environment) are one. The environment is what makes claims upon us, and it is to the environment that we are responsible. Since the environment is the omnipresent God, it is God, "that person to whom violators of our dignity must give an account," who answers the judicial sentiment by being the administrator of justice.(115)

Summarizing the results attained so far by the third method of knowing, Carnell wrote this series of propositions:

> Proposition One: Man is not the author of his own existence. This was the first truth to be proved by moral self-acceptance. Since we are held by powers greater than ourselves, we have no assurance that we will live from one day to the next. We are dependent creatures.
>
> Proposition Two: Analytically included in the relation of dependence is the moral and spiritual environment. We are held by a consciousness of duty from the first moment of moral self-consciousnes. It is impossible to stand in the presence of another person without being confronted by the claims of this environment.
>
> Proposition Three: Analytically included in the moral and spiritual environment is the moral cycle: a consecrated sense of our own spiritual dignity, the obligation of others to accept this dignity, and the guilt of those who abuse or offend us. An aroused judicial sentiment is proof that inconsiderate people are culpable.
>
> Proposition Four: Analytically included in the moral cycle is the judicial predicament. Although we are custodians of the law, we have no authority to enforce the law. But since we continue judging others, we reveal our belief in

> their culpability. And analytically
> included in culpability is the
> obligation to answer to a lawfully
> established tribunal. This is why we
> assert that the very manner of our
> conduct commits us to the reality of the
> administrator of justice.... All of
> this is analytically included in our
> original admission of dependence.(116)

There was little reaction to Carnell's work by those who were not strongly evangelical, yet the response which was forthcoming was generally positive. William A. Mueller was impressed with Carnell's dissection of knowledge into knowledge by inference and knowledge by acquaintance, as well as the distinction Carnell made between knowledge of things and knowledge of persons. On Carnell's treatment of knowledge Mueller offered a compliment: "Here he is close to the best in modern thought as represented by Griesbach, Buber, and Emil Brunner."(117) Roger L. Shinn offered a similar compliment regarding <u>Christian Commitment: An Apologetic</u>.

> One might read the first nine chapters
> of this book and never guess that
> Carnell is a Biblical literalist; and
> the remaining two chapters, although
> more traditional in vocabulary than the
> earlier ones, overlap at many points the
> writings of varied contemporary
> Christian thinkers. Furthermore, the
> authors whom Carnell quotes do not
> belong to any in-group.(118)

The book was "too scholastic in its reasoning and not penetrating enough in its understanding of Scripture" for Shinn, yet he did see that Carnell had made a valuable contribution to the furthering of communication between diverse theological groups.(119) Both of these evaluations of Carnell's work confirm the later assessment of Carnell made by <u>The Christian Century</u> shortly after his death: "Through recent years the editorial staff of the Century has cherished the fact that it had in Dr. Carnell a two-way bridge between itself and one of the more conservative wings of evangelical Christianity."(120)

The only positive evangelical reaction to

Carnell's work came from some of his colleagues at Fuller Theological Seminary who viewed the work as an original contribution to philosophy, one which rivaled the genius of Aristotle or Kant.(121) What these evangelical peers of Carnell realized, along with those non-evangelical contemporaries who reacted positively to Carnell's ethical thought, was that Carnell had succeeded in at least one of his goals. He had developed an epistemology for the moral sense which could be employed by many who called themselves Christian. Although Carnell was an evangelical, he had placed the emphasis in his work not on confession or creed, but rather on passion and commitment. The tool he offered Christendom was usable by all who wanted to develop commitment, irrespective of doctrinal conviction.

The majority of evangelicals who gave attention to Carnell unfortunately were looking for doctrinal errors in his work. One reviewer realized that Carnell was introducing existentialism into evangelicalism, and correctly noted that at the point where existentialism abandons reason Carnell was not existential. He went on to level two doctrinal criticisms. First, he accused Carnell's moral argument in knowledge by moral self-acceptance of advocating a soteriology based upon human goodness. "If he teaches that only men of 'character' can know God, what becomes of the Christian doctrine of the justification of sinners?" Second, he charged that Carnell was not careful enough in his employment of the term "orthodox" to describe his convictions regarding Christianity. Carnell may claim that the Bible is his norm, but unless he defines how the Bible is to be used and understood, his use of the term "orthodox" is nothing but an assertion that his way is the right way.(122)

Gordon H. Clark made two accusations regarding Carnell's theology. He saw, first of all, that Carnell offered a disparagement of foreign missions by arguing that all who believe, not just those who contemplate the atonement, will by saved.(123) Yet in the previous two paragraphs Carnell had argued for the correctness of Christianity as against other religions. Further, in the subsequent paragraphs Carnell made the point that missions are necessary not because of human inability, but because of human inactivity. His emphasis in the entire work was not upon ability, but upon action. "Not that men cannot repent without being confronted by Christ after the flesh, but that they do not repent without such confrontation."(124) Clark erred in his accusation of Carnell because he understood Carnell to be speaking of human nature when in fact Carnell spoke of human activity.(125) Clark's second problem with Carnell was that Carnell, in Clark's estimation, had founded theology upon ethics rather than making ethics derivative from theology. Such a switch of priorities was characteristic of those who, like Mary Baker Eddy or Kant, denied the authority of God's special revelation as found in the Bible. The correct approach to ethics, according to Clark, is to submit to revelation, and then to derive ethics. On this point also Clark failed to understand Carnell's attempt. Carnell realized and built upon the very point Clark made: that not all people submit to special revelation. The solution to the problem, for Carnell, was not to demand submission to revelation, but rather to derive ethics from what is universally human. In theological language, Carnell offered a system which was usable by those who had only general revelation, as well as those who submitted to special revelation. Again, his goal was to further personal spiritual vitality, not widen the gap between those who confessed evangelical Christianity and those who did not.(126)

The errors of Clark's evaluation were repeated by other evangelicals with regard to other doctrines. One reviewer acknowledged that Carnell evidenced a considerable amount of thought and study, but leveled the accusation that Carnell's work was not valid, for not only had he abandoned the Reformed faith by asserting an Arminian anthropology, but he had denied the truth of Scripture by teaching pantheism.(127) Yet another accused him of (1) rejecting Calvinism by asserting that repentance is possible without the influence of the Holy Spirit, (2) overemphasizing God's immanence to the neglect of God's transcendence, (3) holding that evangelical encounter consists of response to rationally-objective evidences when actually it is response to God through Jesus Christ, and (4) using Scripture to support his philosophy when he should be drawing his philosophy from Scripture.(128) What all the evangelical critics failed to realize was that Carnell had not written a theology but rather a workbook. It took the form of intellectual autobiography, but promised the reader that if followed it would lead the reader into the imperative essence. Carnell's goal was not more confessional orthodoxy, but the production of spiritual vitality, the realization of the value of moral action, and the understanding that individuality consists in passionate decision. Had Carnell's critics realized his goal, they may not have erred in their criticisms of his work.

FOOTNOTES

(1)Edward John Carnell, Christian Commitment: An Apologetic (New York: Macmillan, 1957), p. 2.

(2)Ibid., pp. 7-8.

(3)Ibid., p. 8.

(4)Carnell, Christian Commitment: An Apologetic, pp. 2-3.

(5)Soren Kierkegaard, "Concluding Unscientific Postscript," ed. Robert Bretall, A Kierkegaard Anthology (Princeton: Princeton Univ. Press, 1973), p. 226.

(6)Carnell, Christian Commitment: An Apologetic, p. 5.

(7)Ibid., p. 6.

(8)See Edward John Carnell, The Burden of Soren Kierkegaard (Grand Rapids: Eerdmans, 1965), p. 44n, where Carnell wrote,

> Since I have felt that the methodology of existentialism has all too often been left standing without a firm foundation beneath it, I have tried to develop an epistemology (theory of knowledge) to help provide such a foundation. This epistemology, which has much in common with the views of both Socrates and Kierkegaard, appeals to the realities which already hold a person by reason of existence itself.

(9)Carnell, Christian Commitment: An Apologetic, p. 14.

(10)Edward John Carnell, A Philosophy of the Christian Religion (Grand Rapids: Eerdmans, 1960), p. 450.

(11)Carnell, Christian Commitment: An Apologetic, p. 15.

(12)Carnell, A Philosophy of the Christian

Religion, p. 450.

(13) Carnell, Christian Commitment: An Apologetic, p. 17.

(14) Ibid., p. 18.

(15) Ibid., p. 19.

(16) The naturalistic fallacy is the attempt to derive a statement of the nature of good from a statement of a natural property, or to define ethical terms in non-ethical ones. For a discussion of the naturalistic fallacy, see G. E. Moore, Principia Ethica (New York: Cambridge Univ. Press, 1903), Ch. I, Section B, pp. 5-21.

(17) Carnell, Christian Commitment: An Apologetic, p. 21.

(18) Ibid.

(19) Edward John Carnell, An Introduction to Christian Apologetics (Grand Rapids: Eerdmans, 1966), p. 47.

(20) Carnell, Christian Commitment: An Apologetic, p. 269.

(21) Edward John Carnell, The Case for Orthodox Theology (Philadelphia: The Westminster Press, 1959), p. 27; Carnell, An Introduction to Christian Apologetics, p. 46; Carnell, Christian Commitment: An Apologetic, p. 14.

(22) Carnell, Christian Commitment: An Apologetic, p. 10.

(23) Carnell, The Case for Orthodox Theology, p. 87.

(24) Carnell, A Philosophy of the Christian Religion, p. 463.

(25) George J. Stack, Kierkegaard's Existential Ethics (University: The Univ. of Alabama Press, 1977), p. 172.

(26) Soren Kierkegaard, Concluding Unscientific

Postscript, trans. David F. Swenson and Walter Lowrie (Princeton: Princeton Univ. Press for American-Scandinavian Foundation, 1941), p. 170.

(27)Kierkegaard, "Concluding Unscientific Postscript," p. 218.

(28)Ibid., p. 219.

(29)Ibid., p. 208.

(30)Ibid., pp. 214, 216.

(31)Carnell, A Philosophy of the Christian Religion, p. 463.

(32)Carnell, Christian Commitment: An Apologetic, p. 16.

(33)Ibid., p. 17. The meaning of truth as personal rectitude, from the point of view of epistemological methodology, has been developed by Joe E. Barnhart in "The Religious Epistemology and Theodicy of Edward John Carnell and Edgar Sheffield Brightman: A Study in Contrasts" (unpublished Ph.D. dissertation, Boston University, 1964), pp. 145, 146, 150-151. Barnhart pointed out that personal rectitude, for Carnell, was the sum of goodness of character, inward truth, a kind, humble and gentle character, a truth which comes into being through the transformation which accompanies ethical decision, the state of character which results from the acceptance of moral responsibility, and the quality which an honest person possesses. For the present purpose, rectitude may be understood as the comprehension of and commitment to all human obligation, for all of Barnhart's description may be subsumed under this simplified definition.

(34)Ibid., p. 16.

(35)Ibid., p. 13.

(36)Ibid.

(37)Ibid., pp. 14, 16, 24.

(38)Ibid., pp. 21-22.

(39)Kierkegaard, "Concluding Unscientific

Postscript," pp. 207-208.

(40)Kierkegaard, Concluding Unscientific Postscript, pp. 171, 287.

(41)Carnell, Christian Commitment: An Apologetic, p. 16.

(42)Ibid., p. 22.

(43)Ibid., p. 28. Joe Barnhart, in "The Religious Epistemology and Theodicy of Edward John Carnell and Edgar Sheffield Brightman: A Study in Contrasts," pp. 149-150, explained further Carnell's concept of moral self-acceptance. Barnhart stated that moral self-acceptance is the acceptance of the obligation to consider actions; it is inner honesty, it is the acceptance of duty, it is the willingness to be honest. Moral self-acceptance leads to truth as personal rectitude. It allows for the creation of uprightness and character, while rectitude helps moral self-acceptance be more spontaneous and free.

(44)Ibid., p. 24.

(45)Ibid., p. 25.

(46)Ibid.

(47)Soren Kierkegaard, Either/Or, vol. II (Princeton: Princeton Univ. Press, 1946), p. 289.

(48)Carnell, Christian Commitment: An Apologetic, p. 26.

(49)Ibid., p. 27.

(50)Carnell, A Philosophy of the Christian Religion, pp. 455ff.

(51)Carnell, The Burden of Soren Kierkegaard, pp. 166-167.

(52)Ibid., p. 25.

(53)Carnell, Christian Commitment: An Apologetic, p. 74.

(54)Ibid., p. 73.

(55) Ibid., p. 79.

(56) Carnell, *A Philosophy of the Christian Religion*, p. 489.

(57) Ibid., p. 455.

(58) Ibid., p. 457.

(59) Carnell, *The Burden of Soren Kierkegaard*, p. 172.

(60) Carnell, *A Philosophy of the Christian Religion*, p. 258.

(61) Carnell, *Christian Commitment: An Apologetic*, pp. 74, 141.

(62) Ibid., p. 277.

(63) Carnell, *A Philosophy of the Christian Religion*, p. 473.

(64) Carnell, *The Burden of Soren Kierkegaard*, p. 44n.

(65) In the preface to *Christian Commitment: An Apologetic*, p. x, Carnell wrote "If the scientific method clarifies our physical environment, while philosophical method clarifies our rational environment, what method clarifies our moral and spiritual environment? To the best of my present knowledge, none has been developed. The purpose of this book is to devise and apply a method by which an alert individual can acquaint himself with the claims of his environment."

(66) Ibid., p. 75.

(67) *Journals* VIII A4, as translated by Howard and Edna Hong in Soren Kierkegaard, *Works of Love* (New York: Harper & Row, 1962), p. 17.

(68) Kierkegaard, *Concluding Unscientific Postscript*, pp. 232-233.

(69) Kierkegaard, *Either/Or*, vol. II, p. 294.

(70)Kierkegaard, Concluding Unscientific Postscript, pp. 100-101.

(71)Ibid., p. 495.

(72)Alexander Dru, ed., The Journals of Soren Kierkegaard (London: Oxford Univ. Press, 1951), p. 194.

(73)Kierkegaard, Concluding Unscientific Postscript, pp. 30, 118.

(74)Ibid., p. 30.

(75)Ibid., p. 188.

(76)In Concluding Unscientific Postscript, p. 182, Climacus wrote "I contemplate the order of nature in the hope of finding God, and I see omnipotence and wisdom; but I also see much else that disturbs my mind and excites anxiety. The sum of all of this is an objective uncertainty."

(77)Ibid., p. 338.

(78)For discussions of the differences between Kierkegaard and Carnell on rationality and faith, see John Y. May, "Rationality and Objectivity in the Thought of Kierkegaard and Carnell" (unpublished M.A. Thesis, Univ. of Pittsburgh, 1961), pp. 142-145, and John A. Sims, Edward John Carnell: Defender of the Faith (Washington: University Press of America, Inc., 1979), pp. 81-112.

(79)Carnell, Christian Commitment: An Apologetic, p. 79.

(80)Carnell, The Burden of Soren Kierkegaard, p. 115.

(81)Carnell, Christian Commtiment: An Apologetic, p. 78.

(82)Carnell, A Philosophy of the Christian Religion, p. 466.

(83)Ibid., pp. 505-506.

(84)Ibid., p. 489.

(85)Ibid., pp. 473, 479.

(86)Ibid., p. 500.

(87)Ibid., p. 506.

(88)Kierkegaard, Concluding Unscientific Postscript, p. 89.

(89)Soren Kierkegaard, Fear and Trembling, trans. Walter Lowrie (Princeton: Princeton Univ. Press, 1941), p. 78.

(90)In Christian Commitment: An Apologetic, p. 75, Carnell wrote,

> When one examines Kierkegaard's attitude toward the requirement of logical consistency . . . there is good reason to believe that he flagrantly violated this axiom: that a man corrupts his own dignity, and thus lessens the possibility of knowing truth, if his passionate, ethical life is developed in defiance of a calm and unclouded intellect.

In A Philosophy of the Christian Religion, p. 494, he wrote,

> It is extremely difficult to understand why it is necessary to antagonize faith's relation to rational evidences. Kierkegaard started off with a completely false prejudice in supposing that inwardness is jeopardized when the mind is satisfied with the consistency of objective evidences. It is not psychologically true that passionate concern increases in commensurate ratio to objective uncertainty.

(91)Carnell, A Philosophy of the Christian Religion, pp. 453, 473.

(92)Carnell, Christian Commitment: An Apologetic, p. 76.

(93)Carnell, A Philosophy of the Christian Religion, p. 494.

(94)Ibid., p. 475.

(95)Ibid., p. 495.

(96)Carnell, Christian Commitment: An Apologetic, p. 269.

(97)Carnell, A Philosophy of the Christian Religion, p. 449. This same criticism, based upon the authority of the Bible, was made on p. 473.

(98)Carnell, The Burden of Soren Kierkegaard, p. 170.

(99)Kierkegaard, "Concluding Unscientific Postscript," p. 206.

(100)Carnell, Christian Commitment: An Apologetic, p. x.

(101)Ibid., p. 13.

(102)Ibid., pp. 55-56.

(103)Ibid., p. 57.

(104)Ibid., p. 60.

(105)Ibid., pp. 66-67, 69, 68.

(106)Ibid., pp. 83-84.

(107)Ibid., p. 85.

(108)Ibid., pp. 86, 87.

(109)Ibid., pp. 89-90.

(110)Ibid., pp. 90-92.

(111)Ibid., pp. 91, 92-93.

(112)Ibid., pp. 94-96.

(113)Ibid., pp. 112, 97.

(114)Ibid., pp. 103-104.

(115)Ibid., pp. 104-105, 107-108.

(116)Ibid., pp. 102-103.

(117)William A. Mueller, rev. of Edward John Carnell, <u>A Philosophy of the Christian Religion</u> (Eerdmans), <u>The Review and Expositor</u>, Oct. 1952, p. 497.

(118)Roger L. Shinn, rev. of Edward John Carnell, <u>Christian Commitment: An Apologetic</u> (Macmillan), <u>Theology Today</u>, July 1958, p. 278.

(119)Ibid., p. 279.

(120)"Edward John Carnell Dies In California," <u>The Christian Century</u>, May 10, 1967, p. 612.

(121)In two successive issues of <u>Theology News & Notes</u>, a publication of Fuller Theological Seminary, are found these evaluations of <u>Christian Commitment: An Apologetic</u>: "As I read this book, during the weeks that TN&N should have come out, I stood in awe before such original thought. If our generation overlooks this book, I predict that Carnell in the 21st century will not be unlike Kierkegaard in the 20th. Personally, on my shelf, this ranks with Aristotle and Kant" (Vol. 5, no. 1, p. 10 -- unknown author). Wallis A. Turner wrote, "It can be called basic Apologetics, since it goes beyond objection-answering to provide a defense of the faith in terms of original thought. More important, the book can be called Philosophy, since it makes a fresh and major contribution in that field." (Vol. 5, no. 2, p. 8).

(122)James William McClendon, Jr., <u>Pacemakers of Christian Thought</u> (Nashville: Broadman Press, 1962), pp. 27, 28, 30, 31.

(123)Carnell, <u>Christian Commitment: An Apologetic</u>, p. 296.

(124)Ibid., p. 297.

(125)Gordon H. Clark, "Study in Apologetics," rev. of Edward John Carnell, <u>Christian Commitment: An Apologetic</u> (Macmillan), <u>Christianity Today</u>, Sept. 2,

1957, p. 36.

(126)Ibid., pp. 37-38.

(127)Earl E. Zetterholm, rev. of Edward John Carnell, *Christian Commitment: An Apologetic* (Macmillan), *Westminster Theological Journal*, May 1958, pp. 240-246.

(128)C. Stacey Woods, "What Happens in Commitment?," rev. of Edward John Carnell, *Christian Commitment: An Apologetic* (Macmillan), *Eternity*, March 1958, pp. 35-37.

CHAPTER IV

RECTITUDE AND THE LAW OF LIFE

A basic assertion of Carnell's argument was that human nature can best be understood by realizing that it is composed of two distinct essences: the descriptive, which employs the scientific method to make "is" statements about humanity, and the imperative, which depends upon the third method of knowing to make "ought" statements regarding individuals and society. Carnell's development of the third method thus far has resulted in considerable insight into moral self-acceptance, social relations, and the judicial sentiment, all of which are elements of the imperative essence, yet the content of the imperative essence still remains a mystery. The resolution of this mystery is a necessary goal, for as long as the content of the imperative essence remains unknown, the content of rectitude cannot be identified. If rectitude's content is not named, then the individual has no way of evaluating his or her standing before the administrator of justice.

To know the content of the imperative essence, according to Carnell, is to know what we ought to be. By the third method of knowing we can discover the one overall moral norm which is to be life's guiding criterion. "The term 'imperative essence' is nothing but a name for that phase of the moral and spiritual environment which defines a truly upright life."(1) Carnell realized that he had made a major omission in his argument, for he had not clearly developed that phase. He held that we are custodians of the law and not the law's enforcers, but he had not named the law with precision. When others offend us, the judicial sentiment is aroused and we automatically judge them guilty of breaking the law. What is the law, though, which has been broken? Of what is an offender guilty?(2)

The Law of Justice

Carnell's first candidate for the law of life, that law which offenders break, is easily anticipated by a brief review of some of the highlights of his argument thus far. Carnell held that in social relations we are committed to the law of dignity. When others enter the circle of nearness, they must give some sign of their regard for our person. That law was restated in a way that equated dignity with human rights. To show regard for a person's dignity, then, was identical to a respect for his or her rights. Anyone who does not respect the rights of another person is automatically judged guilty by the offended person. The offended moral faculty was defined by Carnell as the judicial sentiment. In doing so Carnell drew legal language into his argument. Toward the end of his argument Carnell pointed out that we are the law's custodians only, not its enforcers. The fact that we remain unmovable in our demand that the guilty pay for their offenses, however, reveals the need for an administrator of justice. Since God is the administrator of justice, the presence of the judicial sentiment shows that we are committed to the same law to which God is committed--the law of justice.

This review makes Carnell's first answer to the question, "By what law do we judge others?" obvious.

> Hardly had I set my mind to the question but what, like a flash, I decided that <u>we judge others by the law of justice</u>. I grounded my confidence in what I felt was a self-evident element in the most routine affairs of life.(3)

That element is the moral cycle just rehearsed. In defining justice he argued for human conformity to the divine view. "Justice pertains to the administration of the right, and God's image in man is the fixed point for defining this administration."(4) His clearest statement was a quote from Aristotle's <u>Nichomachean Ethics</u>, 1131b: "This, then, is what the just is--the proportional."(5) With regard to social relations, justice, for Carnell, was that law which laid out the minimal terms required for society to exist.(6) At this point it appears that Carnell was being influenced by Reinhold Niebuhr, for Niebuhr held that society's highest moral ideal is justice.(7)

There is no way to establish direct Niebuhrian influence upon Carnell, for Carnell did not use Niebuhr as warrant for his arguments, and he rarely acknowledged Niebuhr as a mentor. Only Carnell knew the extent to which he was borrowing from Niebuhrian thought. Yet it does seem that Niebuhr had at least a partial disciple in Carnell, and it will soon be clear that both developed similar convictions regarding primary moral norms.

A substantial case can be made for the view that Carnell, without acknowledging it, was drawing upon Niebuhr. Niebuhr did not accept Kierkegaard without reservation,(8) but did agree with Kierkegaard in places.(9) Carnell stressed this relationship between Kierkegaard and Niebuhr when he attempted to show that Niebuhr either repeated Kierkegaard or built upon him.(10) The similarity between Niebuhr and Carnell, and the influence the former had upon the latter regarding specific elements of moral thought, must be shown primarily by employing a similar device to that used by Carnell in discussing Kierkegaard and Niebuhr: the drawing of parallels in thought. A case for Niebuhrian influence does not need to be based solely upon parallels between Niebuhr and Carnell, however, for in several of his writings Carnell affirmed Niebuhr and acknowledged general indebtedness to him.

Carnell's method of acknowledging Niebuhr was to praise the moments of truth which he found in Niebuhrian thought. He was not like many of his evangelical peers who, having found an element of Niebuhr which was offensive, rejected all of Niebuhr. Rather, Carnell sought to "appreciate how one of the greatest thinkers of our day has applied the Christian faith to prevailing social, political, and economic issues."(11) For Carnell, "Niebuhr may not say the last word on a subject, but what he does say is authentic, germane, and arresting."(12) He was not afraid to indict orthodoxy for what he felt was its great mistake of exclusivism and separatistic attitude, and to embrace neo-orthodoxy instead: "[D]ialectical theology has marshaled a very imposing array of evidence to show that Calvinism greatly errs when it argues that the law of love is only a religious summary of the second table of the Ten Commandments."(13)

Carnell had more than just an intellectual fondness of Niebuhr. It is accurate to say that Carnell was emotionally moved and even inspired by Niebuhr. In the preface to his book on Niebuhr Carnell wrote, "No serious student can rest at ease in Zion after studying Niebuhr. I myself have been made uncomfortable no few times in the preparation of this manuscript."(14) Later, in writing about Niebuhr and

Billy Graham, Carnell openly affirmed Niebuhrian influence.

> I cheerfully acknowledge a personal indebtedness to Reinhold Niebuhr. It was only after I studied Christian realism, long after I graduated from seminary, that I began to sense the power of pride and pretense in my own life.(15)

It is significant that Carnell wrote this acknowledgment in the same year that <u>Christian Commitment: An Apologetic</u>, was published. Introspection was basic to the material in <u>Christian Commitment: An Apologetic</u>, including Carnell's development of the law of life. This introspection took place in the years between the time when Carnell wrote on Niebuhr and when he realized and acknowledged the place of Niebuhr in his thought. It is probable that the moral questioning to which Carnell was exposing himself was informed by Niebuhrian thought, for Niebuhr was prominent in Carnell's intellectual development at the time.

Carnell admired Niebuhr for his forthrightness regarding his convictions. "There are few who are as courageous as he is to defend what is believed to be the truth."(16) Niebuhr's courage served to inspire Carnell to do the same. Such inspiration was a need Carnell had, for, even though he was an evangelical, he was an intellectual bridge between those who were theologically liberal and their conservative counterparts.(17) As such he at times was critical not only of liberalism, existentialism and neo-orthodoxy, but also of orthodoxy. He thus made himself vulnerable to attack from both sides of the theological spectrum. In short, he played a prophetic role. Niebuhr served as a model of integrity for Carnell, a model from which Carnell drew strength.

There were four elements of Niebuhr's thought which Carnell found particularly helpful. Carnell openly affirmed Niebuhr on all four elements. First, Carnell felt Niebuhr was at his best in <u>Pious and Secular America</u>. After acknowledging that he had profited personally from the essays in the book, he went on to assert the truth of Niebuhr's work: "His analysis of pride and pretense is effective because it is true."(18) So impressed was Carnell with Niebuhr that he wished that the essays in the book "were assigned reading for the President of the land, for every member of his cabinet, and for all who have rule over us. The political immaturity of America could stand a heavy dose of Niebuhrian realism."(19)

In addition to finding Niebuhr correct regarding pride, pretense, and the religious complexion of America, Carnell found Niebuhr's criticism of the easy Christian perfectionism asserted by evangelicalism a position made popular by the revivalistic preaching of Billy Graham, helpful to the maintenance of a healthy orthodoxy. Billy Graham, according to Niebuhr, had departed from "the Reformation doctrine that Christians are simultaneously justified and sinful," and was taking orthodoxy with him. In Carnell's estimation, "I believe it would pay orthodoxy to start listening [to Reinhold Niebuhr]." The danger Carnell saw in Graham was that Graham implied that "if a sinner wants to become a skilled diplomat he need only repent."(20) The logical result of Graham's position is that the only thing preventing immediate justice is a refusal to apply Christian principles. Those who hold such a position will soon become impatient, resentful, and finally violent. The great good which Carnell saw in Niebuhr was that the latter, by pointing out the moral limits in both individuals and in history, provided an intellectual cure to the disease of thinking that there was no distinction between justification and sanctification.(21)

Third, Carnell was impressed with Niebuhr's concern for the moral issues of the situation in which he found himself. At a time when evangelicalism was placing such heavy stress upon personal and individual salvation that social problems and collective responsibility were being ignored, Carnell saw in Niebuhr an evidence of faith which, in nineteenth century America, was an indispensible fruit of personal salvation: concern with the moral situation in which the Christian found himself or herself. For Carnell,

> It is this prophetic defiance of religious and moral complacency that keeps Reinhold Niebuhr in the forefront of theology. Orthodox theologians often become so devoted to hallowed forms that they shrink from participating in the modern Christian dialogue. They rarely

> succeed in relating Christianity to the peculiar difficulties rising out of contemporary life.(22)

Carnell found in Niebuhr an example he wanted to emulate, much as he had found in Kierkegaard an example. Kierkegaard served as an example of personal spiritual vitality as opposed to dead confessional orthodoxy, and Niebuhr offered an example of Christian concern for the this-worldly elements of life. In evangelical terms, Niebuhr offered a picture of the fruit of personal salvation.

Finally, Carnell was impressed with Niebuhr's insight into the dynamics of human interaction and the laws which govern moral action. This fourth element of Niebuhrian thought which influenced Carnell contained the other three, but also added to them the development of the law of life, finding its ideal expression in the law of love. In the preface to his book on Niebuhr Carnell wrote,

> [H]is fundamental psychological understanding of the inevitability of pride and egoistic self-assertiveness in all individual and collective expression, . . . plus his excellent expression of <u>agape</u> love as the final definition of the law of life, are, as a whole, both profound and convincing.(23)

It is this development of the law of life which Carnell used, more than any other part of Niebuhr's thought, in the development of his own moral theory. Throughout Carnell's discussions of justice, consideration, and love close parallels to Niebuhr can be seen. It is reasonable, then, to assert that whereas Carnell did not acknowledge Niebuhr throughout his moral theory, nevertheless Niebuhr was highly influential, for Carnell did give general affirmation to Niebuhr's development of the law of life. Parallels to Niebuhr abound in Carnell's development of the same law.

Several elements of Niebuhr's concept of justice emerged as Carnell developed his view of the law of justice. He appealed to human rights when defending his aroused judicial sentiment on an occasion when he was not waited upon by a clerk, even though he had been standing patiently in line. It was the clerk's violation of his rights, Carnell argued, which aroused the judicial sentiment. This appeal was extended to many common life experiences.

> Since we express our dignity through a free pursuit of human rights, whoever violates these rights is guilty of violating our person.. . . We are entitled to such things as a just share of the highway or sidewalk, the privilege of walking through the city park, and a fair slice of the benefits and securities of citizenship.(24)

Carnell's emphasis upon rights appears to have been taken from Niebuhr, who realized that "all systems of justice make careful distinctions between rights and interests of various members of a community.. . . [C]omplex relations, involving more than two persons, require the calculation of rights."(25)

In addition to human rights, Carnell's understanding of justice involved a second Niebuhrian idea, the concept of equality. If a just relation exists between two people, neither has an advantage over, or can take advantage of, the other. The judicial sentiment is aroused if a person in authority treats with favoritism one who is in his or her charge, rather than treating all equally. The one in authority is guilty, for he or she did not have the right to show a preference.(26) Carnell quoted Thucydides as support for his argument, defining injustice as "unfair advantage taken by an equal."(27) Carnell's idea closely resembled Niebuhr's. Notice how Niebuhr combined the element of individual rights with the element of unfair advantage in this description of justice: "The fence and the boundary line are the symbols of the spirit of justice. They set the limits upon each man's interest to prevent one from taking advantage of the other."(28)

The final element of justice which Carnell apparently borrowed from Niebuhr was the balancing of claims, particularly conflicting claims. For Niebuhr,

> Justice requires discriminate judgments between conflicting claims. A Christian justice will be particularly critical of the claims of the self as against the

> claims of the other.... But if the
> claims of the self (whether individual
> or collective) are not entertained,
> there is no justice at all.(29)

Carnell understood the balancing of claims as give-and-take when applied to social conduct. Each party simultaneously makes a demand upon, and receives something from, the other. When this balance is upset, justice no longer exists, and the judicial sentiment is aroused. "If we pay for goods, we demand a just return for our money; if we sign a contract we expect to have its terms honored."(30)

These three elements of human rights, equality, and the balancing of claims make up Carnell's concept of justice. At this point in his thinking, Carnell suggested a summary statement.

> Whatever else may make up the pith and
> marrow of the imperative essence,
> therefore, justice seems to be an
> important ingredient.... [I]f a person
> enters the circle of nearness, he meets
> rectitude, and thus brings the third
> type of truth into being, whenever he
> sees to justice.(31)

It was not long, however, before he began to realize the shortcomings of justice. As his thinking continued to develop, Carnell discovered three problems with asserting that justice is the final moral norm. First, he observed that acts of gross injustice, such as the exploitation of powerless people by a powerful country concerned only with self-interests, often do not arouse in us the judicial sentiment. We may find such acts intellectually challenging or stimulating, but they do not produce moral indignation within us, for they impinge upon our world only in the descriptive realm, not the imperative one. Carnell dismissed this first problem all too easily, classifying it as trivial, for, he argued, "the judicial sentiment is <u>never</u> aroused . . . until others enter the circle of nearness and penetrate our interests. The third method of knowing is valid only under very special conditions."(32) Since distant, exploited people are not in the circle of nearness, they do not arouse the judicial sentiment. It is odd that Carnell's criterion for moral indignation is the physical distance which separates the observer from the action. The question of whether this criterion is a valid one is a question which Carnell did not address.

The second problem with holding that justice is the final moral norm, unlike the first, did not impress Carnell as being inconsequential. He observed that when a group attempts to make a collective decision on some matter of justice, its grasp of the facts is such that the possibility of error is high. In reference to the court he wrote,

> The deliberating jury has a feeling that justice <u>must</u> be done, and it trusts that when the foreman announces its verdict that justice <u>has</u> been done; but the jury is never perfectly certain that its trust and act are coincident.(33)

The difficulty inherent in Carnell's second observation is that it, according to Carnell, contradicts a clear element of the moral experience of each of us. On an individual level we have no trouble in making immediate judgments of guilt against those who violate our dignity. We have no need to deliberate or evaluate evidence. "We enjoy spiritual clairvoyance. No other datum is needed than the sheer presence of another person before us. Either he receives our dignity or he does not."(34) Now if we are so adept at deciding matters of justice on a personal and individual level, Carnell questioned, why does the ability leave us when we attempt to judge in groups? Apparently Carnell did not realize that when a matter is collective rather than individual, it often is not felt in a personal way by the individual group members. His example of juries is an instance of collective matters which are not personal from the point of view of the jurors. They are emotionally detached from the crime, and for that reason evaluate evidence in an intellectual manner. They do not judge on the basis of a defendant's action when in the circle of nearness of the jurors, but on the basis of his or her action when in the circle of nearness of the one against whom the crime was committed. According to his own theory an act must be within the circle of nearness of the individual, that is, personal, for the individual to be able to make an immediate judgment regarding the guilt of an offender of personal dignity. It is consistent with his own theory, then, that collectivities would have difficulty in making judgments regarding justice. To Carnell, however, the difficulty suggested that "we really do not judge others by the law of justice."(35)

A third problem which led Carnell to question the finality of justice as a moral norm was the fact that the accomplishment of justice, if inspired by a motive which is morally reprehensible, arouses the judicial sentiment. If a person accomplishes justice, the matter is not ended. We must inquire as to the person's motive. If that motive is self-seeking, or if justice is accomplished as a matter of necessity, then the act is void of moral worth. Justice must be a fruit of the moral and spiritual environment, not a work inspired by law.

> This is enough to show that the pith and marrow of rectitude is <u>not</u> the mere formal fact of justice. Although rectitude may never exist apart from justice, justice is not necessarily the same thing as rectitude.(36)

The Law of Consideration

In an attempt to identify the law of life with a higher degree of precision, Carnell asked himself if the judicial sentiment is ever aroused when justice is not the issue. If it is, he concluded, then the content of rectitude is more subtle than the law of justice. Upon reflection he concluded that an infinite number of instances can be named where the judicial sentiment is aroused, although justice is not the issue. If, for example, a slow driver will not bear to the right to let us pass, even though he can see us behind him, he is guilty in our judgment, for he arouses within us the judicial sentiment. If we are in a grocery store and want to buy only a quart of milk, yet are not given the opportunity to go through the cash register line first by a woman who has a full cart of groceries, we judge her guilty. Yet what law has she, or the slow driver, broken? Certainly they have not committed injustices, for the driver has the law on his side, and the woman has on her side the commonly-accepted custom that customers are served in order of appearance at the cash register. Yet we cannot help but judge both guilty.

Now that we have cited instances where

> the judicial sentiment is aroused by
> issues other than justice, we have
> convincingly shown that rectitude is
> formed of a more delicate stuff than
> justice. But what is this stuff? And
> how can it be distinguished from
> justice?(37)

Carnell noticed that in the instance where the judicial sentiment is aroused, yet where justice has not been violated, the offended party is very reluctant to rectify the situation. He thought that if he could discover why this reluctance is present, he would have a clue as to the nature of rectitude. Carnell rejected the thought that in such instances we are unsure about our judgment of guilt, for our nobler faculties and men of character condone our judgment. These two elements of support, it will be remembered, were Carnell's original defense for the rightness of our initial judgment of guilt against those who violate our rights. He also rejected the notion that we are reluctant because the matters seem trivial, for "nothing immoral is trivial to an upright person." The reason we hesitate to charge with guilt those who do not violate justice yet offend our judicial sentiment is that "we cannot convince them of guilt unless we exhibit the very moral perfection that we suspect them of violating."(38)

Carnell asserted that the evidence upon which we judge others in these cases, unlike the evidence presented to a jury in a court, is not public and open. We are aware of the evidence, but the guilty party is not. Our task is to acquaint him or her with that evidence. Yet, unless we show him or her our own moral perfection along with the presentation of evidence, he or she will be offended by our judgmental attitude. Desiring not to offend, we hesitate to confront. The problem arises not out of dispute over law, but out of conflict of personal dispositions. One student in a library, for example, may enjoy the sound of the pencil noises against the table, for it gives him or her a feeling of industry. We, however, are disturbed by it, for it disturbs our concentration. If it continues, we cannot help but judge the other person guilty. No individual should continue an action which frustrates another's concentration. We just believe that the one who does continue such an action does not do so out of a malicious motive, but rather because of an innocent error. "His error, of course, is that he approaches the problem by way of his own life, and not by way of others about him. He universalizes from his particular experience."(39) No change will occur until the other student realizes the situation from our point of view. The reasoning which allows him or her to make that realization is the evidence we must present. We must stop short of making the charge of guilt, however, for the other person must break a known law before he or she can be charged with guilt. Carnell was thus led to a conclusion:

> <u>Before we can confront the student with a sense of guilt, we must sincerely believe in his innocence.</u> He will not recognize his duty until we acquaint him with the evidences; but in providing these evidences we must witness to his moral innocence.(40)

At this point Carnell realized a problem in his thought. He had already argued that our mere presence in the circle of nearness obligates another to regard our dignity. His answer, then, to the question of why we need to present evidence regarding our disposition was that we explain only the elements of our dignity which are not revealed by our mere presence. The other person remains obligated to respect those elements of dignity which inhere in us by virtue of the fact that we participate in humanity. Those elements need not be explained. If they are violated, the person is guilty. In presenting such evidence to another, "<u>we merely provide an occasion to reveal whether or not he is already morally related to us.</u>"(41) If the person's response is gracious and sympathetic, then we know that he or she has submitted to the claims of the moral and spiritual environment. If the response is arrogant and selfish, then we know that the person has rejected the environment's claims. He or she is not rightly related to us.

In situations where justice is not the issue, Carnell sought to determine how another is related to him, but from a selfish point of view. His own pleasure was his goal. For example, if he confronted another person in a library with the fact that pencil noises against a table frustrated his ability to concentrate, he did so in order to secure his own interests. His motive was a selfish one. Carnell's thought at this point parallels Niebuhr's concept of mutual love, a type of love which seeks to insure reciprocity from a selfish point of view. Mutual love "seeks to relate life to life from the standpoint of the self and for the sake of the self's own happiness."(42) This relation is the very type which Carnell sought to accomplish when he went to another and confronted him or her with the elements of his dignity which were not revealed by his mere presence.

Carnell warned against charging someone with guilt when we confront him or her with evidences regarding our dignity. Yet we are guilty of making the charge in our minds, and are unable to change our tendency so to do.

> <u>Not only must we assume the innocence of the student before we can confront him with guilt, but we must submit to the grievous fact of our own guilt--the guilt of having judged him on the testimony of insufficient evidence.</u>(43)

Even Carnell's warning appears to have been influenced by Niebuhr,(44) especially when we recall that Carnell affirmed Niebuhr's entire development of love as the law of life. In explaining Niebuhr, Carnell interpreted the law of love as including "tolerance, forgiveness, and pity." It was these qualities which Niebuhr was defending when he issued his warning against a judgmental attitude.(45) Both the approach to others and the warning when making such an approach, then, are Niebuhrian.

In seeking to determine how another was related to him, Carnell honestly sought to provide the other person with an opportunity to reciprocate the good intentions which Carnell initiated. His intent was not exclusively a selfish one.(46) This element of detail is one which Niebuhr pointed out in his development of mutual love. Mutual love is not so coarse as to calculate the level of reciprocity received from another. Rather it is more gracious in that it tends to develop in relationships where reciprocity can be expected to exist.

> Only in mutual love, in which the concern of one person for the interests of another prompts and elicits a

> reciprocal affection, are the social demands of historical existence satisfied.. . . . The self cannot achieve relations of mutual and reciprocal affection with others if its actions are dominated by the fear that they may not be reciprocated. Mutuality is not a possible achievement if it is made the intention and goal of any action.(47)

In Carnell's thought Niebuhr's assumption of reciprocity is demonstrated by believing in another's innocence and by giving him or her the opportunity to respond in graciousness to the evidences regarding the hidden elements of the dignity of an offended person. His presumption was that the one confronted will reciprocate with the same level of graciousness offered by the one doing the confronting.

Carnell's original question when seeking to define the law of life was, "By what law do we judge others?" His initial answer was that we are committed to the law of justice. The shortcomings of the law of justice, however, required him to pursue the matter further. Having analyzed the normal human response to situations in which justice was not the issue, he was in a position to re-ask the question, yet in a form which reflected the analysis. Rather than restating the question in the original form, he decided to include the element of confronting an offending party with evidences. "To what law are we committed when we go to another person and ask a favor of him? This is more pointed because our contact with the moral and spiritual environment is more precise." To answer the question, Carnell developed six interconnected propositions. First, we have an instinctive sense of our own dignity. When that dignity is violated, we do not hesitate in rendering a guilty judgment against the one violating. Second, since each person is unique, dignity includes mysterious and particular elements which are not extremely apparent. Third, when others enter the circle of nearness, they are obligated to accept all elements of our dignity, including the mysterious and particular ones. Fourth, if the other person is to know the mysterious and particular elements, we must reveal those to him or her. Fifth, if we judge another before revealing the mysterious and particular elements, we arouse in him or her the judicial sentiment, for we cannot expect another to respect those elements of our dignity which we do not reveal. Sixth, when we do reveal ourselves, we must communicate both the mysterious and particular elements of our dignity and the fact that we have not prejudged another.(48) We must, in short, look at the situation from the point of view of another. Feeling he was now in a position to answer his question, Carnell made a major assertion.

> "To what law are we committed when we go to another person and ask a favor of him?" The answer is, <u>We are committed to the law of consideration</u>. Unless we meet this law, we will never excite a sense of obligation in him. We suspect him of being inconsiderate of us; but we will never prove it until we are considerate of him.

Consideration, for Carnell, means "to take in the feelings and point of view of others. It means to stand in their place. It means to believe in their innocence until they reveal convincing evidences to the contrary."(49).

Consideration is not a replacement for justice. Rather, the two are complementary. "Although justice is somewhat grosser than consideration, it is nonetheless as much a part of the law of life as consideration. Or rather, consideration overcomes justice by taking in more than justice." Carnell felt that the elements of our dignity which are apparent to another by the mere fact of his or her presence in our circle of nearness, that is, those elements of dignity which are common to humanity, can be satisfied when justice is done. The elements of dignity which are readily apparent correspond to human rights, not human desires. When the mysterious and particular elements are at issue, that is, those elements of dignity which are not common to humanity but rather are unique to an individual, then justice is insufficient. Unique elements of dignity require the exercise of consideration, for individual desires are the issue. "[W]hen our difference from the race is revealed, the judicial sentiment is aroused if those who enter the circle of nearness fail to pass from justice to consideration." Those who see to consideration have already fulfilled justice, for in being sensitive to the unique elements of dignity, the ones which are common to humanity have been regarded. Nobody can treat another as an individual without regarding him or her as a member of humanity. Society, then, is held together by the law of consideration. "The law of consideration places one under an infinite, progressive obligation to a neighbor.. . . So, we conclude: Consideration is more nearly the pith and marrow of the imperative essence than justice."(50)

Carnell appears not only to have been influenced by Niebuhr's understanding of mutual love, but made the same assertion regarding the place of mutual love, which Carnell renamed "consideration," in social relations. For Carnell the highest ethical norm, that which takes into account an individual's differences from the race as well as his or her similarity to it, is the law of consideration. Anyone who reflects upon typical human experience will arrive at the same conclusion. Niebuhr had earlier observed that an individual can find fulfillment only when he or she is intimately related to others. "Love is therefore the primary law of his nature; and brotherhood the fundamental requirement of his social existence."(51) That observation led to his proposition regarding the law of life. "This brotherly relation of life with life is most basically the 'law of life.' It alone does justice to the freedom of the human spirit and the mutual dependence of men upon each other."(52) For both men, then, the idea of interdependence and the need to live harmoniously were fundamental to an ethical approach to social relations. Carnell defined his law of consideration as taking in the feelings and point of view of the other person, maintaining a belief in his or her innocence, whereas Niebuhr had defined the law of brotherhood as "mutual love, . . . the harmony of life with life within terms of freedom."(53)

The primary assertion regarding the law of life led Niebuhr to a secondary assertion, one which grew out of the first one. The fact that human fulfillment can be achieved only through mutual dependence and the harmonizing of life with life requires that these two conditions exist if a meaningful society is to exist.

> From the standpoint of history mutual love is the highest good. Only in mutual love, in which the concern of one person for the interest of another prompts and elicits a reciprocal

> affection, are the social demands of
> historical existence satisfied.. . . All
> claims within the general field of
> interests must be proportionately
> satisfied and related to each other
> harmoniously.(54)

Carnell, it will be remembered, made a similar statement about the need for the law of consideration to be active if society is to be maintained.(55)

In one more Carnellian idea we can see Niebuhr's influence. Niebuhr held that justice both approximates and contradicts mutual love and brotherhood in that it takes into account the interests of all members concerned, but at the same time makes decisions by means of the calculation of rights. In three ways justice is the servant of mutual love. It extends mutual love's feeling of obligation

> from an immediately felt obligation . .
> . to a continued obligation;. . . from a
> simple relation between a self and one
> "other" to the complex relations of the
> self and the "others"; and . . . from
> the obligations, discerned by the
> individual self, to the wider
> obligations which the community defines
> from its more impartial perspective.. .
> . In these three ways rules and laws of
> justice stand in a positive relation to
> the law of love.(56)

In Carnell's thought we find the same idea of the relationship of justice to mutal love reworded in the language of elements of human dignity. The notion that justice is an approximation of mutual love was stated by Carnell as the assertion that the one who sees to consideration has, in doing that, also seen to justice. Niebuhr's justice-as-a-contradiction-of-mutual-love was paralleled in Carnell's idea that the one who accomplishes justice has not necessarily fulfilled the law of consideration. Niebuhr's three ways in which justice serves mutual love are found in Carnell's law that "In every situation where nothing but the formal side of our life is revealed, the moral sense is satisfied with justice,"(57) for Niebuhr's three statements only apply in areas where the individual is formally identical with the race. In the areas where the individual differs from the race, however, Niebuhr's statements are not applicable, for justice cannot approximate consideration. It contradicts consideration, in fact, for in situations where unique and mysterious elements of dignity are at issue, consideration, not mere justice, must prevail if tolerable social relations are to be maintained.

Carnell realized, after developing the law of consideration, that he had not developed the perfect moral response, for although he had accommodated the common elements of human dignity by the law of justice, and had accommodated the unique elements by the law of consideration, his thinking was deficient.

> Here is the crux of the problem: <u>Justice and consideration only answer to as much of our person as we happen to reveal</u>... . But what about the scores of mysteries that lie unrevealed? A moral acceptance of our person must include an acceptance of these mysteries.(58)

These mysterious elements, Carnell argued, are as much a part of human dignity as are the revealed elements. Justice and consideration, therefore, are a part of the law of life, but they do not sum up the law's totality. There must be another virtue which accommodates the unrevealed elements of dignity.

Like rightly-motivated acts of justice, acts of consideration are outward expressions of inward virtue. They are fruits of rectitude. Fruits however, did not satisfy Carnell.

> It ought to be perfectly clear, hence, that if we are ever going to name the pith and marrow of the imperative essence, . . . we must pass from <u>fruits</u> of rectitude (justice and consideration) to the center of rectitude itself (the law of the spirit of life). Since nothing has moral value unless it is done in the right spirit, this "right spirit" must be the illusive stuff we are trying to isolate and name.(59)

The Law of Love

Carnell admitted that justice and consideration may be honest, direct attempts to receive elements of dignity, but he criticized them as being unable to take in the entire mystery of selfhood. According to Carnell, that mystery can only be received by a person when he or she abandons all thought that full self-revelation is possible. "A truly moral individual accepts our lives for what they are, both in the way they are revealed and in the way they are hidden. <u>This is only to say, in other words, that a moral individual is one who loves</u>." Carnell thus equated moral character with love. Love, he felt, fulfills the law without any overt attempts, for love does no wrong to a neighbor. Rather, love limits itself to the extent of the unrevealed mystery of the beloved. "Love fulfills the law without any consciousness of law."(60) Having made such a bold assertion regarding love, Carnell's next step was to relate love to the moral system he had developed.

Near the beginning of the development of his moral system, Carnell succinctly stated his goal:

> We are attempting to discover the content of the imperative essence, in order that we might clarify the moral and spiritual environment. A clarification of this environment, in turn, will clarify our relation to God.(61)

It was only after having developed his entire system that he was willing to assert that he had discovered the pith and marrow of the imperative essence--love.(62) It is only love which confronts us with an eternal task. When the individual turns from love, he or she gives up existence.(63) This is nothing short of affirming that love is the law of life.(64) It and it only is the standard by which those who enter the circle of nearness are judged. "The total effort of the third method of knowing has been directed to a clarification of this one truth." When Carnell perceived that love is the pith and marrow of the imperative essence and that it is the standard by which we judge others, he had effectively summed up his entire ethical theory in one concept--the concept of love. His next statement became a corollary to this perception.

> Since personal rectitude forms the stuff of the third species of truth, and since the third species of truth comes into existence the moment an individual closes the gap between what he is (the descriptive essence) and what he ought to be (the imperative essence), it follows that love comprises the stuff of rectitude, the third type of truth, the imperative essence, the law of life, the moral and spiritual environment, and the essence of God. Love is the univocal element which makes it possible to say "God is good," and "An upright man is good," for good is but another name for love.(65)

We need to understand clearly Carnell's idea of love if we are to understand his moral system. At the point of definition, however, Carnell became resistant, introducing an existential element. He felt that we know what love is from existence itself. "Since we look for others to love us, we already know what love is; and, knowing it, we should acknowledge it."(66) At places in his writing, though, he did yield elements of a definition. In general, he held love to mean all that the Apostle Paul meant in 1 Cor. 13:4-7.(67) In addition, we know from Carnell's idea of the relation of law and love that love is a fruit, not a work, for love fulfills the law without any conscious efforts to do so. Love, thus, "is an affection which carries its own compulsion."(68) At the heart of Carnell's understanding of love is the notion of the interaction of persons, "a vital sharing of natures."(69) In a sentence, "Love is simply spirit entering spirit in fellowship."(70) With approval, Carnell borrowed from Niebuhr, understanding the lover to be one who changes the person-object relationship into a person-person fellowship. In quoting Niebuhr he related the working of love to that of his concept of justice, which regards a person's similarity to the race, as well as to his concept of consideration, which regards a person's uniqueness from the race.

> Real love between person and person is therefore a relationship in which spirit

> meets spirit in a dimension in which both the uniformities and the differences of nature, which bind men together and separate them, are transcended.(71)

It must be stressed, and it should be clear by now, that justice, consideration, and love are not three different moral responses, the one chosen being dependent upon the situation. Carnell does not permit justice to be a sufficient moral response in some situations, consideration in others, and love in still others. Rather, in all situations the morally-upright person will respond with love, for only love fulfills the demands of the moral and spiritual environment. As the law of life, "love enjoins an equal obligation on all men."(72) For Carnell, that obligation is outward evidences of love,(73) specifically, self-sacrifice.

> Love for God is expressed in worship, and love toward man in self-sacrifice....
>
> To live is to love; and perfect love is found only when we know and enjoy God on the one hand and when we live self-sacrificially for one-another on the other.(74)

In some of his later writings, Carnell defended his affirmation of love-as-obligation with his main authority for ethics, the Bible: "Scripture says that our primary business is <u>love</u>."(75) Yet he was somewhat inconsistent with some of his earlier statements when he employed the scriptural imperative.

> In one stroke biblical ethics defines what is doubtless man's most demanding horizontal, moral obligation. A believer is commanded to love his neighbor, not in a wonderful or sacrificial way, but as <u>himself</u>.(76)

The inconsistency may be accounted for in either of two ways. On the one hand, Carnell may have been defining a higher norm of love--"as himself"--for Christians than he defined for general social relations among all people--sacrificial love. On the other hand, although Carnell appears to have been giving his own opinion on the character of love, he may, as he hinted on the following page, have been giving an opinion with which he disagreed--that of Kierkegaard.(77)

If a person considers only justice or consideration when he or she enters the circle of nearness, and does not regard our whole person, we judge him or her guilty, for the judicial sentiment is aroused. We demand a love response from anyone who enters our presence. Justice and consideration do not suffice. "If we are not viewed through the eyes of love, we are being treated as a thing."(78) It was with approval, then, that Carnell quoted Niebuhr: "Love is thus the end term of any system of morals. It is the moral requirement in which all schemes of justice are fulfilled and negated."(79) By that Niebuhr meant that justice is fulfilled by love in that justice is an approximation of love, and that justice is negated by love in that only love, not justice, can be affirmed as the ideal moral response.

Since love is the only moral response which Carnell affirmed, it appears that he had abandoned his development and defense of the judicial sentiment when dignity is violated. Yet, in his thought love and the judicial sentiment were not in conflict, for "an aroused judicial sentiment is but the negative side of love."(80) When we examine the aroused judicial sentiment and the circumstances or actions which offend our dignity, we discover what is not the essence of rectitude. Knowing what that essence is not, we also know what it is, and thus, because love comprises rectitude, we know the essence of love. The aroused judicial sentiment, then, leads us to the negative side of love.

Justice and consideration are not eliminated as moral responses just because the judicial sentiment is aroused when only justice and consideration are present. It is true that only a love response fulfills the demand we make upon a person when he or she enters the circle of nearness, but a love response is not present if justice and consideration are absent. "[W]hoever takes in the hidden phase of another's life must also take in all that is revealed."(81) The three must be present as concentric circles: the smallest is justice, then consideration, then love. Love is the only response we seek, and it cannot be present if justice and consideration are not. Yet justice and consideration, without love, are shorn of moral worth. Love was not everything for Carnell, but where there is no love, he felt there is no value. "The law of love is the greatest of the laws, but it is certainly not the only law. I simply say that nothing has moral value unless it is done out of love."(82)

It is at this point that Carnell's existential approach to love comes to bear, and it is at this point that his theory impinges upon normative questions. Kierkegaard's influence upon Carnell is clearly visible in statements such as these: "As one lives for others, one feels so good inside, so clean, he perceives at once that he is dealing with the very law of his life."(83)

> Since love has no existence apart from an act of love, it is impossible to give a rationally accurate account of its essence. It can be known only as one loves or is loved. Knowledge by inference must yield to knowledge by acquaintance.(84)

For Carnell, talk about love was insufficient to secure moral worth. That talk had to be converted into action. In his later writing he openly affirmed Kierkegaard's thought at this point.

> [T]he ethical self falls short of its duties until it performs works of love.. . . [L]ove and true existence are the same thing, for love is the law of life.. . . [A]n existing individual is not an existing individual unless he engages in works of love.(85)

Carnell then turned to his exemplary moral authority, Jesus Christ. In him, "the third type of truth--truth as personal rectitude--was flawlessly actuated. Jesus did not say, 'I have the truth,' but 'I am the truth' (John 14:6)." In him we see all of the claims of the moral and spiritual environment fulfilled, for "he loved God with all his heart, and his neighbor as himself." This is precisely what Carnell held that a good person should do. Christ is the incarnation of rectitude, and thus is the incarnation of love. "If one wants to know how to regulate himself among men," Carnell asserted, "he should bring his life to the touchstone."(86) With this conclusion reached, Carnell had completed his ethical theory.

Some of the ways in which Carnell's concept of the law of love was influenced by Niebuhr and Kierkegaard have been mentioned. More attention must now be given to the influences of these two men. Carnell made no attempt to hide the fact tht he was impressed with Kierkegaard's development of the concept of love. "Kierkegaard developed the meaning of Christian love with a profundity, thoroughness, and biblical accuracy which, it is no exaggeration to say, surpassed all previous efforts."(87) At another place he wrote, "When he examines the stuff of decision itself, Kierkegaard's insights reach heights of magnificence. He employs the New Testament concept of <u>agape</u> love.. . . Love is the very content of truth itself, for to be inwardly truthful is to love."(88) Throughout his treatment of love Carnell appears to have been especially swayed by the Dane's thinking. The existential element in the definition of love has already been pointed out, as has Carnell's insistence that love be converted from verbiage to action. These ideas were borrowed by Carnell from Kierkegaard's <u>Works of Love</u>. When affirming the Kierkegaardian element of love which he felt expressed Kierkegaard's highest understanding of the nature of love, Carnell wrote that "the ethical self falls short of its duties until it performs works of love."(89) In <u>Works of Love</u> Kierkegaard had expressed this idea regarding Christian duty when writing that it "<u>involves action, not a mere expression about love</u>, not a reflective <u>interpretation</u> of love."(90) Carnell, then, held that we know love not by a definition of love, but by either loving or by being loved. Love's nature and its action, for Carnell, were inseparable. In Kierkegaard's words, "What love does, that it is; what it is, that it does--and at one and the same time."(91) In describing love Carnell placed emphasis upon self-sacrifice. For him perfect love in this world is achieved only when we live sacrificially for others. Although Kierkegaard went into some detail in his discussion of duty being to love others as one loves himself or herself,(92) the self-sacrificial element is evident, and appears to have been the notion of love which Carnell affirmed.

In Carnell's estimation the morally upright person must accept anyone who enters the circle of nearness as he or she is. The task is not to look for a person who is worthy of his or her love, but rather to see anyone who enters the circle of nearness as worthy of that love, and to love him or her in total. All unrevealed elements of dignity, as well as the revealed ones, are affirmed. Love does not calculate, for calculation is the response of a person who is not morally upright.(93) This idea appears to have been taken from Kierkegaard, for Kierkegaard taught that love does not entertain wishes of how the beloved might be changed to be more lovable in the eyes of the one who loves. "[I]t is important that in loving the individual, actual man, we do not slip in an imagined conception of how we believe or might wish this man should be."(94)

Kierkegaard related law and love in much the same way that Carnell later did. "Love," for Kierkegard, "is the fulfilling of the law, for the law is, despite its many provisions, still somewhat indeterminate, but love is its fulfillment."(95) Love is thus the greatest commandment. Carnell repeated this notion in the way he related law and love. Love does not, for Carnell, negate all law, and all law is not included in love. Rather, love is the greatest commandment, and love, because of its all-encompassing nature, fulfills and completes all other laws. In five specific elements of his development of love as the law of life, the existential nature of love, the relation of love to action, love as self-sacrifice, acceptance without calculation, and the relation of law to love as well as his general impression of the nature of love, Carnell gave evidence of having been influenced by Kierkegaard.

As was the case with Kierkegaard, Carnell made no attempt to hide Niebuhrian influence on the topic of love. The opposite, in fact, was the case. Recall that in the preface of his book on Niebuhr he commented more specifically on Niebuhr's development of love:

> . . . his excellent expression of agape love as the final definition of the law of life [is], as a whole, both profound and convincing.

In particular, it was the way Niebuhr related love to human experience which impressed Carnell.

> One can only draw back and admire the magnificent way Niebuhr has succeeded in

> relating the Christian doctrine of love
> to some of the most complex facets of
> the human situation. It is a rare
> individual who manages to remain true to
> so exalted a moral imperative throughout
> an entire system of thought.(96)

That system in general asserted that love is the law of life, one which is inherent in human nature and one which is best obeyed when there is an absence of conscious efforts to obey it.

> <u>Agape</u> is nevertheless the final law of
> human existence.. . . [A]ll human life
> is informed with an inchoate sense of
> responsibility toward the ultimate law
> of life--the law of love.. . . Love is
> indeed the law of life; but it is most
> surely obeyed when we are not conscious
> of obedience to any law.(97)

Love, for Carnell, was the ultimate law of life, for only love takes into account the entire person. Love is not learned, but is known by everyone from experience and by nature. For Carnell, love is a fruit. Efforts to obey the law, however, are works. This concept of fruit and works is the same idea Niebuhr was conveying when he spoke of unconscious obedience as a prime characteristic of love.

Carnell's understanding of love as sacrifice came primarily from Niebuhr. For Carnell life was love, and perfect love is found only through living self-sacrificially for others. The model of such love was Jesus Christ--incarnate love. If one wants to know what perfect love is, he or she should look to Christ. Years before Carnell wrote, Niebuhr had developed the concept of the ultimate norm for ethics as the perfect love seen in Christ. The highest human possibility, wrote Niebuhr, is the "disinterested and sacrificial <u>agape</u>," of Christ. The life of Christ was, for Niebuhr, the prototype of the utlimate virtue, sacrificial love, and was to serve as a model for all people.

> Christ as the norm of human nature
> defines the final perfection of man in
> history. This perfection is not so much
> a sum total of various virtues or an

> absence of transgression of various
> laws; it is the perfection of
> sacrificial love.(98)

Carnell acknowledged Niebuhrian influence on this point of Jesus being the model of love when he wrote, "Niebuhr rightly grounds the motive of love in Jesus Christ."(99)

Niebuhr recognized that sacrificial love, in its perfection, could not be fully implemented in history, and was therefore an impossible possibility in life."(100) Justice, then, must be substituted as a workable approximation of love.

> [I]t is fairly clear that a religion
> which holds love to be the final law of
> life stultifies itself if it does not
> support equal justice as a political and
> economic approximation of the ideal of
> love.(101)

Love does not do away with justice, but rather is "the fulfillment and highest form of the spirit of justice."(102) Carnell, as Niebuhr, did not forgo the need for justice and consideration, but saw them as necessary responses if love was ever to be approximated. The attempt to take in the unrevealed elements of dignity must first take in all revealed elements. When approaching social issues, Carnell, following Niebuhr, realized that justice had to be supported as an approximation of love. "Justice is a child of love.... Concern for justice is a clear sign that the love of Christ is actively at work within the heart of a believer . . . "(103)

Carnell's entire development of the law of life closely parallels Niebuhr's thought and appears to have been highly influenced by Niebuhr. Elements of Niebuhr's thought are seen in the three laws of justice, consideration, and love parallel to Niebuhr's justice, mutual love, and sacrificial love. Those elements include the calculation of rights, the balancing of claims, equality, love and reciprocity, the notion of the ultimate norm for ethics being sacrificial love, the model of the life of Christ, and the relationship of love to justice.

Carnell did not display wholehearted or uncritical

acceptance of Niebuhr. He was quite selective when employing Niebuhrian thought. His criticism of Niebuhr was guided by his conviction, which found expression throughout his ethics, that theology should be usable by the average person on the street:

> When the man on the street asks about the plan of salvation, he receives very little precise guidance from the theology of Reinhold Niebuhr. This, I assert, is the grand irony of Christian realism.. . . When it comes to the acid test, therefore, realism is not very realistic after all.(104)

Carnell made one passing remark regarding the inadequacy of Niebuhr's epistemological and metaphysical support of his brilliant insights into the inevitablity of pride and the nature of love as the law of life,(105) but except for this one statement his criticism of Niebuhr was in three major areas: history, Christology, and bibliology. The criticism of Niebuhr's view of history had two distinct elements. First, Carnell strongly opposed Niebuhr's rejection of the historicity of the resurrection of Christ in lieu of a symbolic interpretation. For Carnell, if the resurrection did not occur in history, then any story about a resurrection is a lie, and as such is useless to produce a faith in the truth, especially for the common person.(106) Second, Nieburh's rejection of the historicity of the biblical Adam and Eve and the fall, as well as the actuality of Adam's headship of the race, was offensive to Carnell. To Carnell Niebuhr's view of Adam, Eve, and the fall removed any need for Christ. If Adam and Eve were not historically sinless until the fall, and if Adam was not the head of the race, the Carnell could not see how the second Adam, Christ, was necessary in order for salvation to be a real possibility for human beings living in history.(107)

Niebuhr's Christology, involving both the person of Christ and the work of Christ, were problematic to Carnell. In one passage Carnell wrote that the evangelical "believes that Niebuhr's view of the person of Jesus is sheer blasphemy." He explained his statement by pointing out what he felt were the errors in Niebuhr's thought. He was most disappointed in Niebuhr's separation of Christ, who is the wisdom of history, from the person of Jesus who walked in Jerusalem. Carnell felt that Niebuhr, reflecting his liberal training, had bifurcated Jesus Christ into an inconsequential historical Jesus and an abstract and symbolic Christ. The result was a theology which was quantitatively, but not qualitatively, different from others. The result, according to Carnell, is the loss of faith. Niebuhr's soteriology was disappointing to Carnell also, for he felt that Niebuhr, as he had done with the person of Christ, had affirmed liberalism's soteriology.(108) For Carnell this affirmation meant the loss of the gospel itself.

> Here, perhaps, is the clearest line of demarcation between orthodoxy and realism.. . . Orthodoxy teaches that Christ propitiated an offended judicial element in the character of God. Realism does not. Moreover, orthodoxy contends that this difference decides the gaining or losing of the Christian gospel.(109)

Carnell's chief criticism of Niebuhr centers on Niebuhr's level of biblical accuracy as well as his attitude towards the Bible. The other two major criticisms find expression in this third criticism. His strongest critique is in the short statement, "Niebuhr's Biblical inaccuracy is unbelievable," and regarding Niebuhr's soteriology Carnell wrote, "If the Bible is right in its structure, then Niebuhr is clearly wrong."(110) There are similar statements elsewhere in Carnell's writings.(111) Regarding Niebuhr's attitude toward the Bible, Carnell understood Niebuhr to be a liberal.

> The Bible contains, not God's plenarily inspired will for man, as in orthodoxy, but rather a salvation history (Heilsgeschichte) which is to be appropriated critically through depth experience.. . . For both liberal and Niebuhr, therefore, the Bible is authoritative only at those points where there shines through a clarification of an experience gained earlier.(112)

In evaluating Niebuhr's approach to the Bible as compared with that of orthodoxy he saw that Niebuhr "judges the Bible by dialectical insights; orthodoxy judges dialectical insights by the Bible."(113) So evil was this inversion to Carnell that it destroyed Christianity. "Niebuhr has so emasculated the Biblical witness in his penchant for the dialectic, that Christianity is robbed of its uniqueness."(114)

It is necessary to assess the significance of Carnell's use and rejection of Niebuhr, as well as Kierkegaard. I choose to reserve this assessment, however, for the concluding statement on the significance of the entire study.

FOOTNOTES

(1)Edward John Carnell, Christian Commitment: An Apologetic (New York: Macmillan, 1957), p. 172.

(2)Ibid., pp. 171-172.

(3)Ibid., p. 172.

(4)Ibid., p. 173.

(5)Richard McKeon, ed., The Basic Works of Aristotle (New York: Random House, 1941), p. 1007, as quoted by Carnell in A Philosophy of the Christian Religion, p. 356.

(6)Edward John Carnell, A Philosophy of the Christian Religion (Grand Rapids: Eerdmans, 1952, p. 276.

(7)Reinhold Niebuhr, Moral Man and Immoral Society (New York: Charles Scribner's Sons, 1942), p. 257.

(8)In Human Destiny, p. 38n, Niebuhr rejects Kierkegaard's appeal to absolute absurdity as a means to the final truth about life, asserting instead that final truth is only a partial absurdity which must transcend the mind's self-centered system of meaning.

(9)See, for example, Niebuhr, Human Destiny, pp. 57, 61.

(10)Edward John Carnell, The Burden of Soren Kierkegaard (Grand Rapids: Eerdmans, 1965), pp. 47, 54, 87, 132; Edward John Carnell, The Theology of Reinhold Niebuhr (Grand Rapids: Eerdmans, 1960), pp. 33, 46, 59, 70-72, 89, 91, 132, 137, 142, 157-159.

(11)Edward John Carnell, "Niebuhrian Apologetic," rev. of Gordon Harland, The Thought of Reinhold Niebuhr (Oxford), Christianity Today, Aug. 1, 1960, p. 34.

(12)Ibid., pp. 34-35.

(13)Edward John Carnell, "Perfect Assurance," rev. of Cornelius Van Til, The Defense of the Faith (Presbyterian and Reformed Pub. Co.), The Christian Century, Jan. 4, 1956, p. 15.

(14) Carnell, The Theology of Reinhold Niebuhr, p. 5.

(15) Edward John Carnell, "Can Billy Graham Slay the Giant?" Christianity Today, May 13, 1957, p. 4.

(16) Carnell, The Theology of Reinhold Niebuhr, p. 5.

(17) "Edward John Carnell Dies in California," The Christian Century, May 10, 1967, p. 612.

(18) Edward John Carnell, rev. of Reinhold Niebuhr, Pious and Secular America (Scribner's), Eternity, Feb. 1959, p. 43.

(19) Ibid.

(20) Edward John Carnell, "A Proposal to Reinhold Niebuhr," The Christian Century, Oct. 17, 1956, p. 1197.

(21) Ibid.

(22) Edward John Carnell, "Can Billy Graham Slay the Giant?" Christianity Today, May 13, 1957, p. 3.

(23) Carnell, The Theology of Reinhold Niebuhr, p. 5.

(24) Carnell, Christian Commitment: An Apologetic, p. 173.

(25) Reinhold Niebuhr, The Nature and Destiny of Man, Vol. II, Human Destiny (New York: Charles Scribner's Sons, 1964), p. 252.

(26) Carnell, Christian Commitment: An Apologetic, p. 173.

(27) Ibid., quoting Thucydides, The Peloponnesian War (Oxford), p. 63.

(28) Niebuhr, Human Destiny, p. 252.

(29) Reinhold Niebuhr, "The Spirit of Justice," Christianity and Society, Summer, 1950, reprinted in D. B. Robertson, ed. Love and Justice (Philadelphia: The

Westminster Press, 1957), p. 28.

(30) Carnell, Christian Commitment: An Apologetic, p. 173.

(31) Ibid., pp. 173-174.

(32) Ibid., p. 174.

(33) Carnell, A Philosophy of the Christian Religion, pp. 356-357.

(34) Carnell, Christian Commitment: An Apologetic, p. 175.

(35) Ibid.

(36) Ibid., p. 176.

(37) Ibid., p. 178.

(38) Ibid., pp. 91, 179.

(39) Ibid., p. 181.

(40) Ibid., p. 182.

(41) Ibid., pp. 182-183.

(42) Niebuhr, Human Destiny, p. 82.

(43) Carnell, Christian Commitment: An Apologetic, p. 184.

(44) John C. Bennett, in his article in Charles W. Kegley and Robert W. Bretall, eds., Reinhold Niebuhr: His Religious, Social and Political Thought (New York: Macmillan, 1956), p. 54, quoted Niebuhr's article in Christianity and Society, Spring, 1938, p. 1, to clarify Niebuhr's warning against self-righteousness: "The real problem for the Christian is not how anyone as good as he can participate in unethical political activity, but how anyone as sinful as he can dare to set himself as a judge of his fellow men."

(45) Edward John Carnell, "Reinhold Niebuhr's View of Scripture," Inspiration and Interpretation, ed. John W. Walvoord (Grand Rapids: Eerdmans, 1957), p. 245.

(46) Carnell, *Christian Commitment: An Apologetic*, pp. 187-188.

(47) Niebuhr, *Human Destiny*, p. 69.

(48) Carnell, *Christian Commitment: An Apologetic*, pp. 172, 189-190.

(49) Ibid., pp. 190-191.

(50) Ibid., pp. 204, 194.

(51) Niebuhr, *Human Destiny*, p. 244.

(52) Ibid., p. 95.

(53) Ibid., p. 78. Freedom, in the sense intended by Niebuhr, referred to the ability to judge good from evil (see p. 95).

(54) Ibid., pp. 68-69.

(55) Carnell, *Christian Commitment: An Apologetic*, p. 194.

(56) Niebuhr, *Human Destiny*, pp. 251-252, 248.

(57) Carnell, *Christian Commitment: An Apologetic*, p. 204.

(58) Ibid., p. 205.

(59) Ibid., pp. 206-207.

(60) Ibid., pp. 207-208, 301.

(61) Ibid., p. 56.

(62) Ibid., p. 208. Carnell reaffirmed this idea in *The Burden of Soren Kierkegaard*, p. 78: ". . . the pith and marrow of ethical duty is love."

(63) Carnell, *The Burden of Soren Kierkegaard*, p. 153.

(64) Carnell, *Christian Commitment: An Apologetic*, p. 295.

(65) Ibid., p. 208.

(66)Ibid., p. 295, 210.

(67)Ibid. Holding that Paul's teaching on love is still normative, Carnell quoted 1 Cor. 13:4-7 as found in the Revised Standard Version:

> Love is patient and kind; love is not jealous or boastful; it is not arrogant or rude. Love does not insist on its own way; it is not irritable or resentful; it does not rejoice at wrong, but rejoices in the right. Love bears all things, believes all things, hopes all things, endures all things.

(68)Ibid., p. 207, 212, 260.

(69)Carnell, The Kingdom of Love and the Pride of Life, p. 126.

(70)Carnell, A Philosophy of the Christian Religion, p. 238.

(71)Reinhold Niebuhr, The Nature and Destiny of Man, Vol. I, Human Nature (New York: Charles Scribner's Sons, 1945), p. 294, as quoted by Carnell in The Theology of Reinhold Niebuhr, pp. 135-136.

(72)Carnell, The Case for Orthodox Theology, p. 63.

(73)Carnell, The Kingdom of Love and the Pride of Life, p. 129.

(74)Carnell, A Philosophy of the Christian Religion, pp. 227-228.

(75)Carnell, The Case for Orthodox Theology, p. 121.

(76)Carnell, The Burden of Soren Kierkegaard, p. 155.

(77)On p. 156 of The Burden of Soren Kierkegaard Carnell wrote, "Let it be borne in mind at all times that we are trying to tell what Kierkegaard said rather than to give our own opinions--here or elsewhere." I am inclined to think that Carnell, rather than disagreeing with Kierkegaard, was defining a higher norm for Christians. This viewpoint was supported later by Carnell's argument in "The Secret of Loving Your Neighbor," Eternity, July 1961, p. 15.

(78) Carnell, Christian Commitment: An Apologetic, p. 209.

(79) Niebuhr, Human Destiny, p. 295, as quoted by Carnell in "Niebuhr's Criteria of Verification," Kegley and Bretall, eds., Reinhold Niebuhr: His Religious, Social and Political Thought, p. 385.

(80) Carnell, Christian Commitment: An Apologetic, p. 209.

(81) Ibid., p. 210.

(82) Ibid. This same idea is found in A Philosophy of the Christian Religion, p. 211.

(83) Carnell, A Philosophy of the Christian Religion, p. 237.

(84) Carnell, Christian Commitment: An Apologetic, p. 210.

(85) Carnell, The Burden of Soren Kierkegaard, p. 167-168.

(86) Carnell, Christian Commitment: An Apologetic, p. 250, 292, 297.

(87) Carnell, The Burden of Soren Kierkegaard, p. 166.

(88) Carnell, A Philosophy of the Christian Religion, p. 464.

(89) Carnell, The Burden of Soren Kierkegaard, p. 167.

(90) Soren Kierkegaard, Works of Love (Princeton: Princeton Univ. Press, 1946), p. 152.

(91) Ibid. p. 227.

(92) Ibid., pp. 15ff.

(93) Carnell, *Christian Commitment: An Apologetic*, p. 209.

(94) Kierkegaard, *Works of Love*, p. 133.

(95) Ibid., p. 85.

(96) Carnell, *The Theology of Reinhold Niebuhr*, pp. 5, 136-137.

(97) Reinhold Niebuhr, *Faith and History* (New York: Charles Scribner's Sons, 1949), p. 175, Reinhold Niebuhr, *An Interpretation of Christian Ethics* (New York: Harper & Brothers, 1935), p. 112, and Reinhold Niebuhr, *Discerning the Signs of the Times* (New York: Charles Scribner's Sons, 1949), p. 185.

(98) Niebuhr, *Human Destiny*, pp. 71, 68.

(99) Carnell, "Niebuhr's Criteria of Verification," p. 386.

(100) Reinhold Niebuhr, *Faith and History* (New York: Charles Scribner's Sons, 1949), p. 175.

(101) Niebuhr, *An Interpretation of Christian Ethics*, p. 131.

(102) Niebuhr, "The Spirit of Justice," p. 25.

(103) Edward John Carnell, "A Christian Social Ethics," *The Christian Century*, August 7, 1963, pp. 979-980.

(104) Carnell, "Can Billy Graham Slay the Giant?," p. 4.

(105) Carnell, *The Theology of Reinhold Niebuhr*, p. 5.

(106) Carnell, *An Introduction to Christian Apologetics*, p. 245, and "Can Billy Graham Slay the Giant?," p. 4.

(107) Carnell, *The Theology of Reinhold Niebuhr*, pp. 132, 137, 142, 145.

(108) Ibid., pp. 156, 144, 198, 200.

(109)Carnell, "Can Billy Graham Slay the Giant?," p. 4.

(110)Carnell, The Theology of Reinhold Niebuhr, pp. 132, 198.

(111)Ibid., pp. 82-83, 89, 158. See also Carnell, An Introduction to Christian Apologetics, pp. 194n, 233-234.

(112)Ibid., p. 57.

(113)Carnell, "Reinhold Niebuhr's View of Scripture," p. 252.

(114)Carnell, The Theology of Reinhold Niebuhr, p. 197.

CHAPTER V

THEORY AND PRACTICE

Carnell had more than just a passing interest in questions of ethical practice. For him the relieving of emergency situations took precedence over the translation of the Bible in the hierarchy of priorities for foreign missionaries.(1) The importance of this notion is realized only when we recall that the primary epistemic moral authority in Carnellian thought, as well as the content of the Christian faith, is the Bible. Ethics, for Carnell, was a practical discipline. It had to do with conduct, not just thought. His law of love had to be understood existentially, for it had no content until it was seen in acts of love. Carnell saw ethics as a normative science, "that branch of learning which defines for man what he ought to do.. . . It prescribes right and wrong conduct." Elsewhere he wrote, "Ethics is the science of conduct. It is that branch of learning which tells a man what ought to be and how he ought to conduct himself."(2)

Coloring his whole approach to ethics was the assumption that there exists a transcendent ethical norm to which all people are subject. Anyone who violates the norm by destroying the lives of others becomes guilty, for the norm defines humanity as it ought to be expressed in action.

> Right and wrong, justice and injustice, thus, are ethical laws written deep in the fabric of the universe. Whereas the laws of physics may change with deeper insights into the nature of the universe, the basic ethical laws of kindness, justice, purity, and holiness will never change. They define man in his changeless nature, themselves being unconditioned by the changing moods of history.(3)

The notion of transcendent, unalterable ethical laws was not inconsistent with Carnell's divine command approach, for he identified them not with platonic ideas, but with the mind of God.(4) It follows, therefore, that the proper ethical standard should be the one which reflects and incorporates the mind of

God. For Carnell, that standard was found in his epistemic and exemplary moral authorities, Scripture and Christ.

> Western culture has succeeded only on the strength of the insight that the will and mind of God, as revealed in the Ten Commandments and in Jesus Christ, can successfully standardize the ethical judgments of men.(5)

Believing that the Bible and the life of Christ are normative for human conduct, Carnell formed a view of how the individual should be involved in social matters.

Carnell asserted that all social relations are founded upon faith.(6) If there is no faith, that is, trust, between members of a group, then the group cannot function as a social unit. Where trust is present, however, there exists the possibility for love between members, for love is based upon trust. The presence of love carries with it an inherent relationship between the lover and the beloved, for "the law of love negates any static subordination of life to life. Human equality is the limiting concept of all Christian social action."(7) The equitable balancing of interests is justice and, in Carnellian thought, is an approximation of the unreachable ideal--love. It was with the notion of justice in mind that Carnell wrote his clearest statement on social ethics, a brief article entitled "A Christian Social Ethics." He started with a definition: "Social ethics deals with the question of just relations between members of a group."(8) Dignity and well-being, according to Carnell, accompany the establishment and maintenance of justice, and diminish with the exercise of injustice. The affirmation of an individual's dignity, it will be recalled, was Carnell's litmus paper of moral uprightness. The one who regards another's dignity demonstrates rectitude; the one who disregards another's dignity reveals his or her moral perversity. The pursuit of justice, then, is imperative if one is to be morally upright. The Bible and the life of Christ require not only faith, but the exercise of the possibility of just action which faith affords.

The duties of an individual member of

> the church include wholehearted support of everything that falls within the cause of the gospel and wholehearted support of everything that falls within the cause of justice. Whenever a believer downgrades justice he offends the whole council of God.. . . The interests of the gospel and the interests of justice are not barbed incompatibles; they are gentle moral correlatives.. . . The one should be done, and the other not left undone.

For Carnell, the two are intertwined, for they both derive their existence from the one source of the love of God revealed in Christ. "The atonement of Jesus Christ was heaven's answer to the just requirements of the law.. . . . Hence the more we honor just relations, the more we bear witness to the divine image in us."(9) The fostering of justice, then, ought to be just as natural for the Christian as missionary activity or preaching, for "concern for justice is a clear sign that the love of Christ is actively at work within the heart of a believer."(10)

In explaining how a Christian is to pursue justice Carnell appealed to his authoritative source, the Bible. He chose the action of the apostles regarding the institution of slavery as an example, and accused those who fault the apostles for their failure to attack slavery as holding "a very unimaginative grasp of Christian social action." Carnell proposed that the apostles attacked slavery the proper way--"with grace and dignity, not grossly and frontally." His reason for affirming such a subtle approach was simple: "the existing order suffered from 'hardness of heart.' Unless social changes are introduced gradually, revolution is invited."(11) Radical social upheaval, for Carnell, was never an allowable approach to social action, for a gospel of revolution, he asserted, would be a gospel of an ideology, not the good news of promised blessings through Jesus Christ.

Let us now turn to an investigation of the application of Carnell's ethics to concrete life situations. At this level Carnell realized that he had left one major difficulty unexplained. His most dominant ethical theme was summed up in his inaugural address as president of Fuller Theological Seminary.

> Here is a truth whose finality no
> Christian is at liberty to deny: "You
> shall love your neighbor as yourself."
> And in this one command we have both a
> final truth and a final reason why we
> are to be tolerant of others.(12)

Since the individual is both commanded to love and capable of loving others, he or she will never find satisfaction until that love is seen in action, for "man is completely man only whenever he loves, shares, and fellowships."(13) In a particular relationship between two individuals love means that each approaches the other with humility, accepting the mystery of the other person. "If this rule is cordially obeyed, vengeance and intolerance will yield to patience and understanding, for love takes in the sanctity of another life and wishes for it nothing but good.(14) It is at this point that the difficulty surfaces. Carnell expressed it this way:

> May a Christian thrust a bayonet through
> the heart of a man and yet retain the
> sweetness and peace of heart which is
> the possession of those who, in
> obedience to God, make the law of
> humility and love their meat?

Just how is the law of love to be applied in complex social situations over which the individual has no control? Does the same ethical norm which governs relationships between individuals govern relationships between nations? Rather than seeking to develop an elaborate system of application in which love could always be held as the only norm before which all moral decisions must bow, Carnell conceded that the implementation of love in all instances was a practical impossibility.

> It is a shocking experience for young
> Christians to realize that they live in
> such a complex social situation that the
> application of the law of love is
> exceedingly difficult, if not
> impossible.(15)

His problem stemmed from a conflict which he saw between what Scripture taught regarding love and nonresistance, on the one hand, and what reason told him regarding the need to resist evildoers in order to preserve freedom and the Christian faith, on the other. His solution shows that he appealed, once again, to Reinhold Niebuhr. That solution was to propose that Scripture teaches that there is complexity within society. "The Scriptures teach that there are three independent spheres in life of which the Christian is simultaneously a member." Those three are the home, the church, and the state. The first two merge into one in some instances, since "family distinctions are lost in the church, as we are all spiritually one in the Lord." What Carnell really proposed, then, was two spheres: personal and political. It must be pointed out that the state, just because it is distinguished from the church is not excluded from the spiritual realm. Rather the government is ordained by God for the purpose of affirming the good and putting down evil. Without government, Carnell asserted, there would be anarchy, a situation which is unacceptable as long as sin lasts and individuals turn from the rule of God. It is necessary, then, for government to set up law, regulation, and order.(16)

Niebuhr's thought became helpful to Carnell at this point. Niebuhr made the observation that the moral dynamics between nations or small groups is different from the dynamics between individuals. The former, by exercise of will alone, is not capable of moral action on as noble a level as is the latter.

> The weaknesses of the spirit of love in solving larger and more complex problems become increasingly apparent as one proceeds from ordinary relations between individuals to the life of social groups. If nations and other social groups find it difficult to approximate the principles of justice, . . . they are naturally even less capable of achieving the principle of love, which demands more than justice.(17)

The solution to the delimma, for Niebuhr, was to assert a lesser norm than love for groups and nations. Only justice, with its coercive element, could maintain a livable social situation.

All social co-operation on a larger

> scale than the most intimate social group requires a measure of coercion.. . . [O]nly a romanticist of the purest water could maintain that a national group ever arrives at a "common mind" or becomes conscious of a "general will" without the use of either force or the threat of force. This is particularly true of nations, but it is also true, though in a slighter degree, of other social groups.(18)

What Carnell did was to borrow from Niebuhr and propose two standards of ethics, one for the family and church, and another for government. He went so far with this idea that he asserted that the government <u>cannot</u> be governed by the same standard under which <u>fall</u> the family and the church.(19)

The only ethical standard which fulfills the demands of an individual vis-a-vis another individual, whether in the family or in the church, is the law of love. Any mere approximation of love, such as the law of justice or the law of consideration, betrays the moral perversity of the one entering the circle of nearness. Carnell summed up this conviction regarding the individual in personal relationships: "In all matters pertaining to personal fellowship, he is governed by a sensitive obedience to the law of love."(20) The meaning of the law of love, for particular situations, Carnell found in his epistemic moral authority. "In both the Old and New Testaments we are commanded to love our neighbor as ourself. This is a specific duty." The duty to love another is based upon the fact of self-love. Self-love is the norm against which action toward a neighbor is measured. The only acceptable action is one which fulfills the Golden Rule, the one by which we do as we would be done by. Just how do we want others to treat us? "We want them to treat us as human beings who are plagued with weakness, prejudice, temptation, dependent love needs, and a host of mysteries which escape precise detection and classification."(21) In short, just as we long for complete acceptance of our total being by those with whom we come in contact, so love demands that we treat others in the same way. Some specific examples will show what complete acceptance of the total being means.

In the case of drunkenness, Carnell affirmed

society's efforts on behalf of alcoholics, holding that the alcoholic, above others, needs help.(22) His attitude was that we must exhibit love by putting ourselves in the place of the alcoholic and asking ourselves how we would want to be treated. "Surely we would not want to be scoffed at by high and mighty Christians."(23) Rather, "the Christian pities the drunkard as a diseased man and seeks every medical and psycho-therapeutic means that modern science, guided by common grace, can proffer." Love does not end with pity, however, but continues on to view the situation from a biblical perspective. The result is the consignment of alcoholism to the realm of sin, and the holding of the alcoholic as responsible for his or her initial surrender to drink. Condemnation of alcoholism must be differentiated from condemnation of the alcoholic, however. Love is not so vicious as to view action and persons as equals. "The drunkard must be pitied as one diseased; but he must be warned as one that has sinned. The Christian must love the drunkard but hate the drunkenness."(24)

A second case is the relationship between love, happiness, and prosperity. Carnell's basic assertion is that "material possessions can bring great joy--provided that they are sanctified by love," for material possessions are not ends. Rather, they are means through which love can work. For example, a family may have no kitchen furniture. Happiness need not be absent, however, for the father can improvise a table and some chairs from old plywood and orange crates. Since it is the father's love for the family which prompts the construction of improvised furniture, happiness can result. The furniture is a means through which love is expressed and happiness is produced. It appears to be a truth, then, that possessions do not, in themselves, produce happiness, but rather happiness is experienced when possessions are shared as an expression of love. "Love releases our hold on goods. When we love, we share.. . . Goods are not enjoyed unless they are shared. And they cannot be shared by a selfish heart."(25) With regard to material possessions, Carnell's norm of loving others after the standard of self-love translates into the free sharing of goods. The result is the production of mutual happiness.

Carnell realized that along with love's happiness and peace comes agony. When two are joined in a love relationship, each feels the pain of the other. When one dies the other, in a sense, dies. This realization led Carnell to be sympathetic to the possibility of euthanasia. "Euthanasia is a live social question because pity in the heart of the lover sometimes expresses itself in the destruction of the beloved's consignment to physical existence."(26) To love another means to accept the other's complete person, including both revealed and unrevealed elements of dignity. In Carnell's mind the affirmation of dignity apparently allowed for the possibility of the destruction of physical torment.

In the final example we see that Carnell approached the issue of television and its use in society largely from a positive perspective, for he saw television as a means by which love could be expanded throughout the world. This could be accomplished in two ways: through the breaking down of prejudice and through the expansion of the circle of nearness. The breaking down of the prejudice could be facilitated by juxtaposing nations intimately with each other on the video screen. The citizens of each nation could then observe the cultural patterns of other nations. The result would be an increase in international understanding to the point that the customs of each nation would become the common knowledge of all other nations.(27) Citizens of each nation, acting out of knowledge rather than ignorance and prejudice, would be more willing to accept the dignity of citizens of other nations. Love on an international scale thus would be increased. In a similar manner Carnell envisioned television as a means to expand the circle of nearness of virtually any individual. "Ideally directed, TV can move man out of his sinful isolation and place him face to face with the world outside where the barbed and thorny human drama is being played." Recall that if a person or situation is not within the circle of nearness, judicial feelings are not aroused. If a tragedy is half way around the world, it concerns us very little. Television, however, can bring into any home an earthquake in China or the concentration camps of Germany. It can, in short, expand the circle of nearness to encompass the entire world. That expansion may draw out of formerly-complacent individuals "a deeper accentuation of love and sympathy.. . . Most men are more than ready to weep with those that weep."(28)

Carnell anticipated no challenge to his assertion

that in the personal sphere the law of love is the standard which all action should seek to implement. Both family and church relationships are to be governed by the law of love. Following Niebuhr, however, he realized that the government has less ability to incorporate love in its actions than do individuals. In addition, Carnell made explicit his idea that personal conduct must be distinguished from official, that is, government, conduct.(29) Of the political sphere, then, he was led to ask, "by what standard is the government ruled?"(30) Should the standard be love, or should it be some other norm?

Carnell reasoned that if one made the mistake of assuming that the state is bound by the same law, in its actions, as are individuals in theirs, some foolish and regrettable implications are necessitated. Rather than making that mistake, we must realize a basic truth in speaking about the state as a morally-responsible body: the state is impersonal. "The obvious reason for impersonality in government is that the larger ego lacks the very organs of sensitivity required for love." The government, he asserted, is not a person, but instead is "a thing, a relation, a center of power, a collective ego, an 'Uncle Sam,' an arm of strength, a rallying center for the interests and vitalities of a people."(31) Love by nature, however, must involve persons, for it requires the sharing of spirits out of a sense of sacrifice and humility. Since an impersonal entity, such as the government, has no spirit and cannot be humble, it cannot love. It follows that the government's moral norm cannot be the law of love. What, then, can it be, and how is that norm to be discovered?

Since the government is an impersonal thing, it is of a different category from the individual, who is a person. The government's larger collective ego, Carnell reasoned, is one step removed from the individual's smaller personal ego. "[I]t follows that the ethical code which defines its obligations is likewise one step removed from the ethic of love." Love, it will be remembered, took into account those elements of dignity which made a person a distinct individual. The particular and mysterious elements of dignity were the concern of love. It was for that reason that Carnell declared love to be a higher norm than justice, which respected only those elements of dignity which are common to humanity. The impersonal body cannot view people as distinct individuals, for it is unable to see them as anything other than the impersonal entity, humanity. In its actions it can do no other than preserve humanity as a mass, and thus it seeks not to affirm particular individuals in distinction from the mass, but rather affirms the mass as an impersonal body. The only way that this affirmation can occur is by the implementation of the law of justice. "Justice is a negative statement of the law of love; it is that ethic which forbids a person to transgress the rights of others,"(32) that is, the mass. The individual who feels that his or her government is acting out of a sense f justice, rather than love, will not have the judicial sentiment aroused, as in the case when he or she feels that another person in the circle of nearness is responding only with justice. The reason for this is that the one in whose circle of nearness another enters expects to interact with that other on the highest moral level of which he, she, or it is capable. If another person enters the circle, then love is expected. If, however, the government, which is capable only of justice, enters the circle, then only justice is expected. "In every situation where nothing but the formal side of our life is revealed, the moral sense is satisfied with justice."(33)

The Christian lives in both the personal and the political sphere. As regards his or her involvement in each, how are the two ethical norms to be implemented? Carnell summarized his position by asserting that government is God-ordained for the purpose of rendering vengeance against those who seek to destroy justice. The ruler is a good ruler if he or she maintains justice alone, for the law of love is not applicable in the political sphere. When the Christian is in a position to act as an agent of the government, "being armed with power to represent this impersonal mind, he stands under orders to discharge the rule of justice." The Niebuhrian influence is strong here for, just like Niebuhr, Carnell held that in inter-personal situations the Christian is to act with love, but in political or social situations the law of justice is the moral norm to be implemented. As long as the government is seeking to implement justice, the Christian is to be a faithful citizen.(34) Notice that Carnell put a stipulation on the Christian's submission to the state: the state must be on the side of justice. The important point was not government qua government, but government qua agent of justice. If the government was not serving justice, then it was not fulfilling its God-ordained function, and the Christian was no longer under obligation to obey.

> Nations as well as individuals can be good or bad, worthy or unworthy. It is the irresponsible, emotional mind, not the thoughtful citizen, who cries "My country, right or wrong." If an <u>individual</u> may be right or wrong, so may the state.(35)

Carnell illustrated the interactions of the law of love and the law of justice with two instances in which the Christian may be involved. Consider the situation in which a Christian police officer happens upon the scene of a robbery. How does he implement both love and justice in the situation, since he finds himself both in a personal relationship with the robber and in an official relationship as an arm of the law? Carnell's answer was that the officer should both weep and shoot. The tears express love for the robber, and the gun executes justice and preserves the peace. Consider a second situation. A Christian judge presides over a court. How can both sacrificial love and the law of justice be met? "As a man, he pities; as a judge, he condemns."(36) The judge must have no malice in his heart, however, for such evil intention would violate the law of love. The obvious problem with Carnell's approach is that on the official level nobody is responsible. If the government is an impersonal "it," then it can never be held accountable for its actions, for only persons can be held accountable. In Carnell's scheme there are no persons in government, for every participant in official action is merely an agent, an arm, with no mind. The mind becomes relevant only in personal action. In official action, however, there is no mind, but merely a machine which implements justice. The result is that government is granted great license and is easy prey to corruption by those who would use the impersonal for their own personal gain.

The law of justice in official action was applied by Carnell to two specific issues: war and capital punishment. War, Carnell felt, was "the most exasperating social order to which the Christian must adjust his new life," for it is a result of a sinful world order. The approach to ethics which takes into account different spheres, however, will help the Christian solve the problem of his or her involvement in war. Only the double standard of the law of love, in personal affairs, and the law of justice, in official action, can account for all the biblical teaching regarding both nonresistance of enemies and submission to the government. The law of love requires that the Christian carry no malice in his or her heart toward the soldiers of an enemy nation. Justice, however, requires that the Christian soldier execute judgment against those who transgress justice. If the soldier hates the enemy, then he or she is not a good citizen of heaven, for God's standard for individuals is love. If the soldier refuses to kill the enemy, however, then he or she is not a good citizen of the world, for the government is God-ordained and the Christian is to submit to those actions which the government deems are in the interest of justice. The result is that the soldier

> trips the lever which opens the bomb door effecting the instant death of a hundred thousand people. As the bombs fall, the Christian bombardier has a personal love in his heart for those about to die, wishing that he were dropping Bibles for their salvation rather than lethal sticks for their destruction.(37)

Carnell was quick to follow this statement with an assertion of one condition, the need that "the government be on the side of righteousness before a Christian can conscientiously fight." This means that the only war in which a Christian may participate is a defensive one, for "defensive warfare is simply the use of a national police force to destroy gangsterism on an international scale." The soldier is in the same position as is the police officer at the robbery--both need to stop injustice with force. Since government's task is to promote justice by stopping those who seek personal gain through injustice, the Christian can never participate in a preventive or aggressive war, for such wars do not fall under the category of justice. If a police officer may not shoot someone who may possibly rob a bank, then the soldier may not fight an enemy which may possibly commit an injustice.(38) When the pacifist realizes the truth of the concept of the spheres, Carnell argued, then he or she will realize that it is his or her duty to fight in a defensive war, for to fight is merely "to defend with arms the elect of Christ."(39)

The second issue to which Carnell applied the law of justice was capital punishment. He anticipated the objection to capital punishment which applied to Jesus' teaching regarding love of enemies and nonresistance by drawing in his concept of the spheres. "[T]his appeal is irrelevant, for Jesus is speaking about personal, not official conduct. The civil magistrate, let us remember, is an officer." To Carnell, then, the matter became one of justice, not love. He allowed for humanitarian efforts, such as attempts to make prisons humane and the welcoming of ex-convicts back into society, but these efforts, he felt, were secondary to the cause of justice. He found his defense in his exemplary moral authority, the life of Christ.

> A Christian should have little difficluty grasping this, for his own salvation rests upon a public act of legal punishment. Christ did not die merely to set a moral example. He died to propitiate divine justice.

In an initial response to the question of the Christian's stand on capital punishment, then, Carnell responded: "he should take a stand for justice." Once guilt is determined, the Christian should not hesitate in dispatching the demands of justice. He or she should not resist out of concern for arguments which are not based upon justice, such as the notion that capital punishment is not a deterrent or the facts that wealthy people have an advantage in court, minority groups experience discrimination, leniency is shown toward women, particularly pretty ones, and innocent people are often condemned. Such arguments are beside the point, for the prime consideration must be justice. The civil penalty must be executed. It is clear that for Carnell there was only one answer to the question of when capital punishment would be administered. "Capital punishment should be administered whenever justice requires it." Specific crimes which Carnell felt justify the penalty of death include "treason in time of war, conspiracy to kill an officer of the law, multiple murder, or a crime against humanity."(40)

FOOTNOTES

(1)Edward John Carnell, A Philosophy of the Christian Religion (Grand Rapids: Eerdmans, 1952), p. 454.

(2)Edward John Carnell, Television--Servant of Master? (Grand Rapids: Eerdmans, 19500, pp. 116-117, 16-17.

(3)Ibid., pp. 17-18, 19-20.

(4)Carnell, A Philosophy of the Christian Religion, p. 127. "Western culture is founded on the faith that there is an archetypal world of truth, goodness, and beauty which stands over history as its changeless norm. Plato called it the world of Ideas; Christianity calls it the mind of God."

(5)Carnell, Television--Servant or Master?, p. 19.

(6)Carnell, A Philosophy of the Christian Religion, p. 29.

(7)Edward John Carnell, The Case for Orthodox Theology (Philadelphia: Westminster, 1959), p. 56.

(8)Edward John Carnell, "A Christian Social Ethics," The Christian Century, Aug. 7, 1963, p. 979.

(9)Ibid.

(10)Ibid., p. 980.

(11)Carnell, The Case for Orthodox Theology, p. 62.

(12)Edward John Carnell in "The Glory of a Theological Seminary" (Inaugural Address as President of Fuller Theological Seminary), May 17, 1955.

(13)Carnell, Television--Servant or Master?, p. 36.

(14)Carnell, "The Glory of a Theological Seminary," p. 16.

(15)Edward John Carnell, "Should a Christian Go to

War?" His, April 1951, p. 5.

(16) Ibid., p. 6.

(17) Reinhold Niebuhr, Moral Man and Immoral Society (New York: Charles Scribner's Sons, 1947), pp. 74-75.

(18) Ibid., pp. 3, 6.

(19) Carnell, "Should a Christian Go to War?", p. 6.

(20) Ibid., p. 7.

(21) Edward John Carnell, "The Secret of Loving Your Neighbor," Eternity, July 1961, p. 15.

(22) Edward John Carnell, "Is Drunkenness a Sin?" United Evangelical Action, March 1, 1948, p. 6.

(23) Carnell, "The Secret of Loving Your Neighbor," p. 16.

(24) Carnell, "Is Drunkenness a Sin?", p. 8.

(25) Edward John Carnell, "Personal Happiness and Prosperity," Christian Economics, Sept. 3, 1957, p. 4.

(26) Carnell, A Philosophy of the Christian Religion, p. 252.

(27) Carnell, Television--Servant or Master?, p. 58.

(28) Ibid., pp. 65, 66.

(29) Edward John Carnell, Christian Commitment: An Apologetic (New York: Macmillan, 1957), p. 192n.

(30) Carnell, "Should a Christian Go to War?", p. 6.

(31) Ibid., p. 7.

(32) Ibid.

(33) Carnell, Christian Commitment: An Apologetic, p. 204.

(34)Carnell, "Should a Christian Go to War?", pp. 7, 8.

(35)Carnell, Television--Servant or Master?, pp. 18-19.

(36)Carnell, "Should a Christian Go to War?", pp. 7, 8.

(37)Ibid., p. 5, 8.

(38)Ibid., pp. 8, 10.

(39)Edward John Carnell, An Introduction to Christian Apologetics (Grand Rapids: Eerdmans, 1948), p. 321.

(40)Edward John Carnell, "Capital Punishment and the Bible," Eternity, June 1961, pp. 19, 32, 20.

CONCLUSION

In this study we have seen Carnell as a member of the evangelical tradition of social ethics in this country. Additionally, we have discovered his authority for ethics, investigated his ethical theory, and seen how he put that theory into practice. Carnell's work must now be evaluated from the standpoint of significance.

It appears odd that Carnell would choose Kierkegaard and Niebuhr for his mentors. As an evangelical we would expect him to select from within his own theological persuasion, rather than that of existentialism and neo-orthodoxy. Carnell's choice, however, reveals one of his basic convictions, one which is key to an understanding of his significance. At the time Carnell was writing an evangelical was characterized primarily as one who subscribed to the basic beliefs of fundamentalism: (1) the verbal inerrancy of the Scriptures, (2) the diety of Jesus, (3) the virgin birth of Christ, (4) the substitutionary atonement of Christ, and (5) the physical resurrection and bodily return of Christ. Yet to be accepted within the evangelical community one had to do more than just affirm the fundamentals. He or she had to affirm certain individuals and repudiate others. Not only did evangelicalism's content have to be embraced, but so did its community. It was this dual embrace which Carnell felt was wrong. For him the only test for religious orthodoxy was submission to biblical authority. "Orthodoxy is friendly toward any effort that looks to Scripture; it is unfriendly toward any that does not."(1) It was because of this conviction regarding Scripture's authority that he felt free to criticize not only theologians such as Karl Barth, but also conservatives such as Billy Graham and J. Gresham Machen.(2) It was because of this same conviction that he felt free to draw from Kierkegaard and Niebuhr, for at the points where he used them he felt that they were more true to the teaching of Scripture than was anyone else. Their general association with existentialism and neo-orthodoxy did not prevent Carnell from using the portions of their thought which he felt to be compatible with orthodoxy.

In using Kierkegaard and Niebuhr, Carnell offered to evangelicalism a new intellectual stance. In his evaluation of fundamentalism he stressed the fact that one of fundamentalism's prime characteristics is intellectual stagnation.(3) Of orthodoxy he wrote that it

> <u>tries</u> to relate Scripture to the more technical phases of science and philosophy, but its efforts are seldom very profound. Orthodoxy does not know enough about modern presuppositions to speak with authority. Publishers confront such a paucity of first-rate orthodox literature that they must fill out their lists by reprinting the works of older apologists and divines.(4)

Carnell's use of Kierkegaard and Niebuhr gave to evangelicalism a model of sound scholarship and made the statement to non-evangelicals that evangelicals were capable of careful thought in the realms of philosophy and theology. His attempt was to return academics to evangelicalism and evangelicalism to the theological and philosophical forum. As aids to both efforts he could pick no better mentors than Kierkegaard and Niebuhr.

Carnell realized that even though the evangelical community was not authoritative, he participated within that community by choice. He knew that he needed to identify with a particular group if he was to gain an audience, and that he would lose that audience if, in his writings, he gave too much affirmation to what the audience denied. We have seen that Carnell was very hesitant to affirm Niebuhr openly and, to a lesser extent, Kierkegaard. The reason for this hesitation lies in this notion of author-audience rapport. The audience's attitude toward Kierkegaard and Niebuhr can best be understood by examining some of the writings of other leading evangelicals. Carl Henry expressed three of evangelicalism's problems with Niebuhr. First, Niebuhr set himself against evangelical ethics:

> The transition from the Social Gospel to Niebuhrian ethics marked at one and the same time a perpetuation of the revolt against historic evangelical ethics and a continuance of many of the socio-economic emphases spawned by the Social Gospel.

Second, Niebuhr substituted existentialism for biblical authority.

> Niebuhr formulated his views . . . not in the context of the ontological categories of Biblical Christianity, which he rejected, but rather in terms of subjective categories of his own, and in an existential framework of theology unfamiliar to the Biblical writers.

Third, Niebuhr rejected the church's highest priority.

> [T]he Niebuhrian dismissal of the social significance of individual regeneration and sanctification signaled an unjustifiable defection from the primary task of the church in the world, that of the spiritual evangelization of unregenerate humanity.(5)

Chester E. Tulga expressed more of evangelicalism's frustrations with Niebuhr in his book, The Case Against Neo-Orthodoxy. Even the title conveyed the attitude that all of neo-orthodoxy should be rejected by evangelicals. Tulga emphasized two points, however. First, he rejected Niebuhr's symbolic interpretation of the resurrection and classified Niebuhr as unbiblical.

> This entire teaching on the resurrection and the interpretation of the resurrection story is foreign to the New Testament and must be rejected by the Christian believer as vain philosophy rather than sound theology.

Second, Tulga attacked Niebuhr's thinking on eschatology.

> Reinhold Niebuhr . . . thinks that Jesus and Paul were in error concerning the return of the Lord.. . . The Neo-Orthodox do not accept the New Testament apocalyptic teachings, and regard the historical Jesus to be in error on these matters.(6)

Henry and Tulga made similar criticisms of

Kierkegaard's thought. Henry denounced Kierkegaard for his revolt against reason in matters of ethical decision and accused him of rejecting the inspired and authoritative Scripture.(7) Tulga also indicted Kierkegaard for his rejection of reason and accused him of being not a theologian or expositor of the Bible, but rather a frustrated genius who substituted irrationalism for sound theology.(8)

Although most of evangelicalism called for a general rejection of existentialism and neo-orthodoxy, it is clear that the majority of evangelicalism's criticisms revolved around the five fundamentals. What Carnell did was to reject Niebuhr and Kierkegaard at the same points where the rest of evangelicalism rejected them--where their writings contacted the fundamentals. The exception was that both evangelicalism and Carnell were also critical of Kierkegaard's stance on the role of reason in ethical decision and commitment. On this exception, as was the case of evangelicalism's criticisms of Niebuhr's and Kierkegaard's departure from the fundamentals, Carnell concurred with other evangelicals. Where Carnell did not follow most of evangelicalism was in the fact that he did not reject all of Niebuhr and Kierkegaard for denying the content of the fundamentals. He was knowledgeable enough to realize that not all moral and theological truth is based upon the fundamentals: in fact, much of it is not. In his own affirmation of the fundamentals, however, Carnell clearly established himself within the community of evangelicalism, and thus secured for himself an audience. It was to this audience that he had to tailor his writing.

This discussion of community and audience raises the question of why Carnell was reluctant to acknowledge strongly and clearly the influence of Niebuhr, and to a lesser degree Kierkegaard, throughout his writings. It is clear that Carnell was writing to an audience which had very little sympathy for either of Carnell's mentors. Kierkegaard was not as threatening to evangelicals as was Niebuhr because he was not a contemporary. Niebuhr, however, was both alive and present in the American theological situation, and as such represented a greater present danger than did Kierkegaard. Both men, though, were viewed by evangelicalism as being opposed to the gospel and enemies of God.

It was into the hostile evangelical environment that Carnell tried to introduce Kierkegaard and Niebuhr with the goal of having their constructive ideas incorporated into the moral understanding of that group. Since Carnell's emphasis was on ideas rather than people, that is, content rather than community, he had no great need to have evangelicalism accept Kierkegaard and Niebuhr as people, but only to accept their ideas. In addition, Carnell realized that if he were to stress too heavily Kierkegaard and Niebuhr as people, rather than stress their ideas, evangelicalism would be inclined not to accept Kierkegaard and Niebuhr as being compatible with evangelical thinking on ethics, but instead to reject Carnell as incompatible for being Kierkegaardian and Niebuhrian. Carnell's solution to the issue was freely to use Kierkegaard and Niebuhr, but to give sparing acknowledgment to their influence upon his thinking. In so using Kierkegaard and Niebuhr, Carnell helped return scholarship to evangelical moral thought and gave to evangelicals a window to current moral thinking which had been lacking since before the days of the fundamentalist-modernist controversy.

Even though more than twenty-five years have passed since Carnell wrote his ethics, there are some good reasons why evangelicals should not continue to relegate his work to the dusty shelves of theological library basements. Evangelicalism today needs to do serious thinking about how to make moral decisions, not just which decisions should be made. The simple appeal, "The Bible says so," certainly is an inadequate answer to the question of why one option should be chosen over another. Yet most of modern evangelicalism's ethics rests upon that one appeal. What Carnell offers to evangelicalism is not a replacement of that appeal, but rather an expansion of it and an addition to it. If evangelicals wish to be more relevant both to the world social situation as well as to the academic discipline of ethics, it would pay them to give attention to what Carnell offers them.

First, Carnell offers a model of interaction with non-evangelicals. Much of evangelicalism is still in the emotional position in which it found itself in Carnell's day. Anyone who does not offer whole-hearted affirmation of the fundamentals is totally rejected as a source of any truth whatsoever. What Carnell realized was that not all truth is to be found in

Scripture and that truth, wherever it may be found, has its source in God. As such it should be embraced, not rejected. The Christian Century was correct when it judged Carnell to be a bridge between liberalism and conservativism. Today evangelicals should adopt Carnell's stance, seeking to mend division rather than to solidify it. Sound scholarship, in cooperation with those of different theological persuasions, should be pursued, uncertainties should be admitted, and conflicts should be resolved.

Second, Carnell offers an ethic based upon Scriptural authority but not limited to biblical legislation. Carnell chose Kierkegaard and Niebuhr partially because he felt their developments of love as an ethical norm were absolutely true to the biblical concept of agape. Yet in choosing them his ethic went beyond the technical meaning of the word to the incorporation of existentialism into orthodoxy. Carnell did not deny the confessional aspect of orthodoxy, but rather defended it. He realized, however, that individual moral decision could not be replaced by an affirmation of the creed, but itself needed expression within orthodoxy. By introducing existentialism he attempted to create that expression.

Third, Carnell offers a moral epistemology which incorporates and expands upon the biblical material. If the Bible offers no specific guidance on a particular question, many evangelicals are frustrated as to the means of making a decision. In his development of the third way of knowing and the law of life Carnell offers a method of thinking which goes beyond the finding of specific answers in the sacred text to the consideration of typical human moral experience, human nature, inherent human rights, and various moral responses, all of which, together with the Scriptures, should inform the evangelical's moral decisions. It is only through such an individual wrestle with Scripture, human nature and experience, and individual situations that passionate ethical decision can be produced. Evangelicals get passionate about evangelism not by reciting the great commission of Matthew 28, but by individual, active participation in the work of evangelism. In a similar manner, passion about ethics is not produced by reciting biblical teaching on the nature of the good, but by individual struggle with what it means to demonstrate the lordship of Christ in particular moral situations.

What Carnell offers to evangelicals is a method by which the struggle can commence. If evangelicalism is to have a positive effect upon the world situation, and if it is to demonstrate that it follows its Lord by being passionately concerned with the present needs of humanity, as well as the future needs, then it would do well to listen to Carnell.

FOOTNOTES

(1)Edward John Carnell, The Case for Orthodox Theology (Philadelphia: Westminster, 1959), p. 13.

(2)See Edward John Carnell, "Barth as Inconsistent Evangelical," The Christian Century, June 6, 1962, pp. 713-714, "A Proposal to Reinhold Niebuhr," The Christian Century, Oct. 17, 1956, pp. 1197-1199, and The Case for Orthodox Theology, pp.114-117.

(3)Carnell, The Case for Orthodox Theology, pp. 119-120.

(4)Edward John Carnell, "Can Billy Graham Slay the Giant?" Christianity Today, May 13, 1957, p. 4.

(5)Carl F. H. Henry, A Plea for Evangelical Demonstration (Grand Rapids: Baker Book House, 1971), pp. 31, 33, 34.

(6)Chester E. Tulga, The Case Against Neo-Orthodoxy (Chicago: Conservative Baptist Fellowship, 1951), pp. 42, 43-44.

(7)Carl F. H. Henry, Christian Personal Ethics (Grand Rapids: Baker Book House, 1977), pp. 117-118, 135, 137.

(8)Tulga, The Case Against Neo-Orthodoxy, pp. 17-18, 20, 60.

BIBLIOGRAPHY

Primary Sources

Bretall, Robert W., ed. The Empirical Theology of Henry Nelson Wieman. New York: Macmillan, 1963.

Carnell, Edward John. "Barth as Inconsistent Evangelical," The Christian Century, June 6, 1962, pp. 713-714.

_____. "Being-in-Grace," Rev. of Edward Farley, The Transcendence of God: A Study in Contemporary Philosophical Theology (Westminster). The Christian Century, Dec. 14, 1960, pp. 1470-1471.

_____. "Beware of the New Deism," His, Dec. 1951, pp. 14-16, 35-36.

_____. "Billy Graham and the Pope's Legions," Christianity Today, July 22, 1957, pp. 20-21.

_____. "Bowing to Authority." Rev. of Cornelius Van Til, The Case for Calvinism (Baker). The Christian Century, March 10, 1965, p. 304.

_____. The Burden of Soren Kierkegaard. Grand Rapids: Eerdmans, 1965.

_____. "Can Billy Graham Slay the Giant?" Christianity Today, May 13, 1957, pp. 3-5.

_____. "Capital Punishment and the Bible," Eternity, June 1961, pp. 19-20, 32.

_____. "The Case for Orthodox Theology," Christianity Today, April 27, 1959.

_____. The Case for Orthodox Theology. Philadelphia: Westminster, 1959.

_____. "Christendom's Key Issue," Christianity Today, Oct. 12, 1959, pp. 29-30.

_____. "The Christian and Television," His, May 1950, pp. 1-3, 6.

_____. Christian Commitment: An Apologetic. New York: Macmillan, 1957.

_____. "A Christian Social Ethics," The Christian Century, Aug. 7, 1963, pp. 979-980.

_____. "The Concept of Dialectic in the Theology of Reinhold Niebuhr," Unpublished ThD dissertation, Harvard Divinity School, 1948.

_____. "Conservatives and Liberals Do Not Need Each Other," Christianity Today, May 21, 1965, pp. 874-876.

_____. "Criterion of Love." Rev. of Nels F. S. Ferre, Know Your Faith (Harper). Christianity Today, Aug. 29, 1960, pp. 42-43.

_____. "Curious Balance." Rev. of Robert Clyde Johnson, Authority in Protestant Theology

(Westminster). The Christian Century, Dec. 16, 1959, p. 1471.

_____. "Cycle of Confrontation." Rev. of George S. Hendry, The Holy Spirit in Christian Theology (Westminster). The Christian Century, Nov. 21, 1956, pp. 1359-1360.

_____. "Disorder, A Sign of Life." Rev. of Robert McAfee Brown, The Spirit of Protestantism (Oxford). Christianity Today, June 5, 1961, pp. 33-34.

_____. "Erotic Candor." Rev. of Otto A. Piper, The Biblical View of Sex and Marriage (Scribner's). Christianity Today, Feb. 13, 1961, pp. 49-50.

_____. "Evil--Why?" Eternity, Dec. 1960, pp. 22-24, 31.

_____. "The Fear of Death," The Christian Century, Jan. 30, 1963, pp. 136-137.

_____. "For a Better Understanding of the R.S.V." Rev. of Harold Lindsell, ed., Harper Study Bible (Harper and Row). Christianity Today, Feb. 12, 1965, p. 38.

_____. "For Unlazy Critics." Rev. of James Oliver Buswell, Jr., A Systematic Theology of the Christian Religion (Zondervan). Christianity Today, Feb. 26, 1965, pp. 39-41.

_____. "The Glory of a Theological Seminary." Pasadena: Fuller Theological Seminary, 1970.

_____. "Goldwater: Yes or No?" The Christian Century, July 8, 1964, p. 881.

_____. "A Gospel of Despair." Rev. of Jean-Paul Sartre, The Devil and the Good Lord (Knopf). Christianity Today, June 6, 1960, pp. 37-38.

_____. "The Government of the Church," Christianity Today, June 22, 1962, pp. 18-19.

_____. "The Grave Peril of Provincializing Jesus," The Pulpit, May 1951, pp. 2-4.

_____. "Has the Queen Abdicated?" Rev. of William Hordern, New Directions in Theology Today, Vol. I: Introduction (Westminster), and Carl E. Broaten, New Directions in Theology, Vol. II: History and Hermeneutics (Westminster). Christianity Today, Nov. 25, 1966, pp. 28-29.

_____. "How Every Christian Can Defend His Faith: I," Moody Monthly, Jan. 1950, pp. 312-313, 343.

_____. "How Every Christian Can Defend His Faith: II," Moody Monthly, Feb. 1950, pp. 384-385, 429-431.

_____. "How Every Christian Can Defend His Faith:

III", Moody Monthly, March 1950, pp. 460-461, 506-507.

_____. An Introduction to Christian Apologetics. Grand Rapids: Eerdmans, 1948.

_____. "Is Drunkenness a Sin?" United Evangelical Action, March 1, 1948, pp. 6, 8.

_____. "Jesus Christ and Man's Condition," Encounter, Winter 1960, pp. 52-58.

_____. The Kingdom of Love and the Pride of Life. Grand Rapids: Eerdmans, 1960.

_____. "Men Are Not God." Rev. of H. Richard Niebuhr, Radical Monotheism and Western Culture (Harper). Christianity Today, Jan. 30, 1961, p. 32.

_____. "The Nature of the Unity We Seek," Religion in Life, Spring 1957, pp. 191-199.

_____. "New Opportunities to Broaden Your Outlook," The Opinion, May 1967, pp. 3-6.

_____. "Niebuhrian Apologetic." Rev. of Gordon Harland, The Thought of Reinhold Niebuhr (Oxford). Christianity Today, Aug. 1, 1960, pp. 34-35.

_____. "Orthodoxy and Ecumenism," Christianity Today, Sept. 1, 1958, pp. 15-18, 24.

_____. "Orthodoxy: Cultic vs. Classical," The Christian Century, Mar. 30, 1960, pp. 377-379.

_____. "Pealism and the Like." Rev. of Donald Meyer, The Positive Thinkers (Doubleday). The Christian Century, Aug. 11, 1965, pp. 990-991.

_____. "Perfect Assurance." Rev. of Cornelius Van Til, The Defense of the Faith (The Presbyterian and Reformed Publishing Co.). The Christian Century, Jan. 4, 1956, pp. 14-15.

_____. "Personal Happiness and Prosperity," Christian Economics, Sept. 3, 1957, p. 4.

_____. "Philosophy and Theology." Rev. of R. M. Hare, Freedom and Reason (Oxford Univ. Press), Yves R. Simon, A General Theory of Authority (Univ. of Notre Dame Press), James Collins, Three Paths in Philosophy (Regenery), Karl Barth, The Great Promise (Philosophical Library), Robert W. Bentram, ed., Theology in the Life of the Church (Fortress), J. P. Mackey, The Modern Theology of Tradition (Herder & Herder), Thomas F. Torrance, Karl Barth: An Introduction to His Early Theology, 1910-1931 (S.C.M. Press), and Joseph E. O'Neill, ed., The Encounter With God (Macmillan). The Christian Century, July 3, 1963, pp. 861-862.

_____. A Philosophy of the Christian Religion.

Grand Rapids: Eerdmans, 1952.

_____. "A Post-Fundamentalist Faith," The Christian Century, Aug. 26, 1959, p. 971.

_____. "The Problem of Religious Authority," His, Feb. 1950, pp. 6-9, 11-12.

_____. "The Problem of Verification in Soren Kierkegaard." Unpublished PhD dissertation, Boston University, 1949.

_____. "A Proposal to Reinhold Niebuhr," The Christian Century, Oct. 17, 1956, pp. 1197-1199.

_____. "Sacraments as Revelation." Rev. of Donald M. Baillie, The Theology of the Sacraments (Scribner's). Eternity, Aug. 1957, p. 26.

_____. "Science and Religion." Rev. of Aldert Van Der Zeil, The Natural Sciences and the Christian Message (T. S. Denison and Co.). Christianity Today, July 18, 1960, pp. 33-34.

_____. "The Secret of Loving Your Neighbor," Eternity, July 1961, pp. 15-16.

_____. "Shaky Foundation." Rev. of W. Norman Pittenger, The Word Incarnate (Harper). Christianity Today, Nov. 7, 1960, pp. 42-43.

_____. "Should a Christian Go to War?" His, April 1951, pp. 4-8, 10.

_____. Television--Servant or Master? Grand Rapids: Eerdmans, 1950.

_____. "The Theological Horizon--By Telescope." Rev. of Nels F. S. Ferre, Searchlights on Contemporary Theology (Harper). Christianity Today, July 3, 1961, p. 32.

_____. The Theology of Reinhold Niebuhr. Grand Rapids: Eerdmans, 1951.

_____. "The Third Day: Jesus and the Multitudes," Los Angeles Times, Mar. 24, 1959.

_____. "A Trilogy of Protestant Theology," The Journal of Bible and Religion, Oct. 1959.

_____. "Two in One." Rev. of Markus Barth and Vern H. Fletcher, Acquittal by Resurrection (Holt, Reinhart & Winston). The Christian Century, Feb. 19, 1964, p. 241.

_____. "Understanding Karl Barth." Rev. of Karl Barth, The Word of God and the Word of Man (Harper Torchbooks), Eternity, Feb. 1958, p. 43.

_____. [Untitled]. Rev. of Alan Richardson, The Gospel and Modern Thought (Oxford Univ.Press). The Westminster Theological Journal, Nov. 1950, pp. 51-57.

_____. [Untitled]. Rev. of Baker's Dictionary of

_____ Theology (Baker). Christian Herald, July 1960, n.p.

_____. [Untitled]. Rev. of Henry Zylstra, Testament of Vision (Eerdmans). Religion in Life, April 1959, pp. 313-314.

_____. [Untitled]. Rev. of Herman Wouk, This is My God (n.p.). Christianity Today, July 6, 1959, n.p.

_____. [Untitled]. Rev. of J. M. Spier, Christianity and Existentialism (The Presbyterian and Reformed Publishing Co.). The Westminster Theological Journal, May 1954, pp. 202-205.

_____. [Untitled]. Rev. of Paul Tillich, Theology of Culture (n.p.). Christianity Today, July 6, 1959, n.p.

_____. [Untitled]. Rev. of Reinhold Niebuhr, Pious and Secular America (Scribner's). Eternity, Feb. 1959, pp. 42-44.

_____. [Untitled]. Rev. of Richard R. Niebuhr, Resurrection and Historical Reason (Charles Scribner's Sons). The Gordon Review, Summer 1958, p. 90.

_____. "The Virgin Birth of Christ," Christianity Today, Dec. 7, 1959, pp. 9-10.

_____. "When Logic Has Gone." Rev. of James A. Overholser, A Contemporary Christian Philosophy of Religion (Regnery). Christianity Today, May 7, 1965, pp. 35-36.

_____. "Why Neo-Orthodoxy?" The Watchman-Examiner, Feb. 19, 1948, pp. 180-181.

_____. "Zen's Voidness." Rev. of Chang Chen-Chi, The Practice of Zen (Harper). Christianity Today, Oct. 10, 1960, p. 41.

Fey, Harold Ed., ed. How My Mind Has Changed. Cleveland: The World Publishing Co., 1961.

Kegley, Charles W., and Bretall, Robert W., eds., Reinhold Niebuhr: His Religious, Social and Political Thought. New York: The Macmillan Co., 1956.

Secondary Sources

Adelmann, Frederick J. S.J., ed. Authority. The Hague, Netherlands: Martinus Nijhoff, 1947.

Allen, E. L. Kierkegaard: His Life and Thought. London: Harper and Brothers, 1935.

Baker, J. P. Rev. of Edward John Carnell, The Burden of Soren Kierkegaard (Paternoster). The Churchman, Autumn, 1966, pp. 244-245.

Barnhart, Joe E. "The Religious Epistemology and Theodicy of Edward John Carnell and Edgar Sheffield Brightman: A Study in Contrasts." Unpublished PhD dissertation. Boston University, 1964.

Becker, William H. Rev. of Edward John Carnell, The Burden of Soren Kierkegaard (Eerdmans). Interpretation, July 1966, pp. 350-351.

Berger, Peter L. The Precarious Vision. Garden City: Doubleday & Co., Inc., 1961.

Bower, Richard Allen. "Lament," The Opinion, May 1967, pp. 1-2.

Brandt, Richard B. Ethical Theory: The Problems of Normative and Critical Ethics. Englewood Cliffs: Prentice-Hall, Inc., 1959.

Brown, J. A., "The Second Advent and the Creeds of Christendom," Bibliotheca Sacra, XXIV, pp. 629-651.

Brown, James. "The Knowledge of God and Natural Theology," The Opinion, May 1967, pp. 7-9.

Carlfelt, C. G. Rev. of Edward John Carnell, The Theology of Reinhold Niebuhr (Eerdmans). The Lutheran Quarterly, Aug. 1952, pp. 339-340.

Carlyon, J. T. Rev. of Edward John Carnell, The Theology of Reinhold Niebuhr (Eerdmans). The Journal of Religious Thought, Spring-Summer, 1953, pp. 163-164.

Clark, Gordon H. "Study in Apologetics." Rev. of Edward John Carnell, Christian Commitment: An Apologetic (Macmillan). Christianity Today, Sept. 2, 1957, pp. 36-38.

Cobb, John B. Jr. "A Panorama of Theologies." Rev. of Edward John Carnell, The Case for Orthodox Theology (Westminster). Interpretation, Jan. 1960, pp. 94-96.

Cole, Charles C. Jr. The Social Ideas of the Northern Evangelists, 1826-1860. New York: Columbia Univ. Press, 1954.

Cruickshank, Andrew. "The Existentialist." Rev. of Edward J. Carnell, The Burden of Soren Kierkegaard (Paternoster). Church Quarterly Review, Jan-Mar., 1967, pp. 102-103.

Daniels, W. H., ed. Moody: His Words, Works and Workers. New York: Nelson & Philips, 1877.

Dayton, Donald W. Discovering an Evangelical Heritage. New York: Harper & Row, 1976.

Demarest, Gary W. Rev. of Edward John Carnell, The Burden of Soren Kierkegaard (Eerdmans). Theology News & Notes, 12, No. 1, pp. 6-7.

Douglas, J. D., ed. The New International Dictionary of the Christian Church. Grand Rapids: Zondervan, 1974.
Dru, Alexander, ed. The Journals of Soren Kierkegaard. London: Oxford Univ. Press, 1951.
Durkheim, Emile. The Division of Labor in Society. New York: The Free Press, 1964.
"Edward John Carnell Dies in California," The Christian Century, May 10, 1967, p. 612.
Finney, Charles G. Lectures on Revivals of Religion. Cambridge: The Belknap Press of Harvard Univ., 1960.
Foreman, Kenneth J. Sr., Rev. of Edward John Carnell, The Case for Orthodox Theology (Westminster). Theology Today, Oct. 1959, pp. 402-404.
Frankena, William K. Ethics. 2d ed. Englewood Cliffs: Prentice-Hall, Inc., 1973.
Graham, Billy. World Aflame. Garden City: Doubleday & Co., 1965.
Grounds, Vernon C. "Take Another Look at S. K." Rev. of Edward John Carnell, The Burden of Soren Kierkegaard (Eerdmans). Christianity Today, Feb. 18, 1966, pp. 33-34.
Gustafson, James M. "The Place of Scripture in Christian Ethics: A Methodological Study," Interpretation, 24.
Haines, Aubrey B. "Edward John Carnell: An Evaluation," The Christian Century, June 7, 1967, p. 751.
Halverson, Marvin, and Cohen, Arthur A., eds. A Handbook of Christian Theology. Cleveland: World, 1958.
Harris, R. Baine, ed. Authority: A Philosophical Analysis. University: The University of Alabama Press, 1976.
Harrison, Everett F., Bromiley, Geoffrey W., and Henry, Carl F. H., eds. Baker's Dictionary of Theology, Grand Rapids: Baker, 1960.
Henry, Carl F. H. Aspects of Christian Social Ethics. Grand Rapids: Eerdmans, 1964.
_____. Christian Personal Ethics. Grand Rapids: Baker Book House, 1977.
_____. A Plea for Evangelical Demonstration. Grand Rapids: Baker Book House, 1971.
_____. The Uneasy Conscience of Modern Fundamentalism. Grand Rapids: Eerdmans, 1947.
Hordern, William E. A Layman's Guide to Protestant Theology. revised ed. New York: The Macmillan Co., 1973.

Hughes, Philip E. "Defending the Faith." Rev. of Edward John Carnell, The Case for Orthodox Theology (Westminster). Christianity Today, Jan. 4, 1960, pp. 42-43.
Jewett, Paul K. "An Appreciation Given at Dr. Carnell's Funeral on April 28, 1967," The Opinion, May 1967, p. 17.
Kierkegaard, Soren. Concluding Unscientific Postscript. Princeton: Princeton Univ. Press, 1944.
_____. Either/Or, Vol. II. Princeton: Princeton Univ. Press, 1946.
_____. Fear and Trembling. Princeton: Princeton Univ. Press, 1941.
_____. Works of Love, Princeton: Princeton Univ. Press, 1946.
Klassen, Harry. "An Open Letter," The Opinion, May 1967, p. 6.
Knudsen, Robert D. Rev. of Edward John Carnell, The Kingdom of Love and the Pride of Life (Eerdmans). Westminster Theological Journal, Nov. 1961, pp. 109-111.
Lawson, Lewis A., ed. Kierkegaard's Presence in Contemporary American Life: Essays From Various Disciplines. Metuchen: The Scarecrow Press, Inc., 1971.
Lewis, Gordon R. Testing Christianity's Truth Claims. Chicago: Moody Press, 1977.
Magnuson, Norris. Salvation in the Slums: Evangelical Social Work, 1865-1920. Metuchen: The Scarecrow Press, 1977.
May, John Y. "Rationality and Objectivity in the Thought of Kierkegaard and Carnell," Unpublished MA thesis, Univ. of Pittsburgh, 1961.
McCasland, S. Vernon. Rev. of Edward John Carnell, The Theology of Reinhold Niebuhr (Eerdmans). The Journal of Bible and Religion, Oct. 1951, pp. 216, 218.
McClendon, James William Jr. Pacemakers of Christian Thought. Nashville: Broadman Press, 1962.
McKeon, Richard, Ed. The Basic Works of Aristotle. New York: Random House, 1941.
McLoughlin, William G., ed. The American Evangelicals, 1800-1900. New York: Harper & Row, 1968.
Miller, William. Evidence from Scripture and History of the Second Coming of Christ, About the Year 1843. n.c.: n.p., 1836.
Minnema, T. The Social Ethics of Reinhold Niebuhr: A Structural Analysis. n.c.: J. H. Kok N. V.

Kampen, 1958.
Moberg, David O. *The Great Reversal*. revised ed. Philadelphia: A. J. Holman Co., 1977.
Moody, Dale. Rev. of Edward John Carnell, *The Case for Orthodox Theology* (Westminster). *Review and Expositor*, April 1960, pp. 205-206.
Moore, G. E. *Principia Ethica*. New York: Cambridge Univ. Press, 1903.
Mueller, William A. Rev. of *A Philosophy of the Christian Religion* (Eerdmans). *The Review and Expositor*, Oct. 1952, pp. 495-498.
Nash, Ronald H. *The New Evangelicalism*. Grand Rapids: Zondervan, 1963.
Nicholas, Robert E. Rev. of Edward John Carnell, *The Case for Orthodox Theology* (Westminster). *Westminster Theological Journal*, Nov. 1959, pp. 88-95.
Niebuhr, Reinhold. *Discerning the Signs of the Times*. New York: Charles Scribner's Sons, 1949.
─────. *Faith and History*. New York: Charles Scribner's Sons, 1949.
─────. *An Interpretation of Christian Ethics*. New York: Harper and Brothers, 1935.
─────. *Moral Man and Immoral Society*. New York: Charles Scribner's Sons, 1960.
─────. *The Nature and Destiny of Man*. Vol. I, *Human Nature*. New York: Charles Scribner's Sons, 1964.
─────. *The Nature and Destiny of Man*. Vol. II, *Human Destiny*. New York: Charles Scribner's Sons, 1964.
O'Doolus, Onesimus. Rev. of Edward John Carnell, *The Case for Orthodox Theology* (Westminster). *Theology News & Notes*, 6, No. 3, pp. 6-8.
Osborn, Andrew R. *Christian Ethics*. London: Oxford Univ. Press, 1940.
Ramm, Bernard. *Types of Apologetic Systems*. First Ed. Wheaton: Van Kampen, 1963.
Rice, John R. "Fuller Seminary's Carnell Sneers at Fundamentalism." Rev. of Edward John Carnell, *The Case for Orthodox Theology* (Westminster). *The Sword of the Lord*, Oct. 30, 1959, pp. 1, 7, 11.
Robertson, D. B., ed. *Love and Justice*. Philadelphia: The Westminster Press, 1957.
Rolston, Holmes. Rev. of Edward John Carnell, *The Kingdom of Love and the Pride of Life* (Eerdmans). *Interpretation*, July 1961, p. 374.
Rose, Ralph A. Letter, *The Christian Century*, Nov. 21, 1956, p. 1363.
Sailer, William S. "The Role of Reason in the

Theologies of Nels Ferre and Edward J. Carnell."
Unpublished STD dissertation. Temple University,
1964.
Sanders, Jack T. Ethics in the New Testament.
Philadelphia: Fortress Press, 1975.
Schoonhoven, Calvin R., and Morgan, Jaymes P. Jr. "An
Appreciation," The Opinion, May 1967, pp. 18-19.
Shein, Louis. Rev. of Edward John Carnell, Christian
Commitment: An Apologetic (Macmillan). The
Journal of Bible and Religion, April 1958, pp.
169-170.
Shinn, Roger L. Rev. of Edward John Carnell, The
Theology of Reinhold Niebuhr (Eerdmans). Theology
Today, May 1951, pp. 284-285.
Sims, John A. Edward John Carnell: Defender of the
Faith. Washington: University Press of America,
Inc., 1979.
Sittler, Joseph. The Structure of Christian Ethics.
Baton Rouge: Louisiana State Univ. Press, 1958.
Smith, Timothy L. Revivalism and Social Reform.
Baltimore: The Johns Hopkins University Press,
1980.
Smith, W. Robert. "To Conquer Rebellion." Rev. of
Edward John Carnell, The Kingdom of Love and the
Pride of Life (Eerdmans). Christianity Today, May
8, 1961, pp. 43-44.
Stack, George J. Kierkegaard's Existential Ethics.
University: The University of Alabama Press, 1977
_____. On Kierkegaard: Philosophical Fragments.
Atlantic Highlands: Humanities Press, 1976.
Stead, William T. Life of Mrs. Booth. New York:
n.p., 1900.
Theology News & Notes. Pasadena: Fuller Theological
Seminary, 1, No. 1, pp. 1-2.
Theology News & Notes. Pasadena: Fuller Theological
Seminary, 1, No. 2, pp. 1-4.
Theology News & Notes. Pasadena: Fuller Theological
Seminary, 1, No. 3, pp. 1-6.
Theology News & Notes. Pasadena: Fuller Theological
Seminary, 2, No. 1, pp. 1-3.
Theology News & Notes. Pasadena: Fuller Theological
Seminary, 2, No. 3, p. 1.
Theology News & Notes. Pasadena: Fuller Theological
Seminary, 2, No. 4, pp. 1-2.
Theology News & Notes. Pasadena: Fuller Theological
Seminary, 4, No. 1, pp. 1-4.
Theology News & Notes. Pasadena: Fuller Theological
Seminary, 5, No. 1, p. 10.
Theology News & Notes. Pasadena: Fuller Theological

Seminary, 5, No. 2, pp. 2, 8.
Theology News & Notes. Pasadena: Fuller Theological Seminary, 13, No. 2, p. 3.
Theology News & Notes. Pasadena: Fuller Theological Seminary, 16, No. 1, p. 9.
Thomte, Reidar. Kierkegaard's Philosophy of Religion. Princeton: Princeton Univ. Press, 1948.
Tulga, Chester E. The Case Against Neo-Orthodoxy. Chicago: Conservative Baptist Fellowship, 1951.
Walvoord, John W., ed. Inspiration and Interpretation. Grand Rapids: Eerdmans, 1957.
Weld, Theodore Dwight. The Bible Against Slavery. Detroit: Negro History Press, 1970.
Wood, A. Skevington. Rev. of Edward John Carnell, The Burden of Soren Kierkegaard (Paternoster). The Evangelical Quarterly, April-June, 1967, pp. 110-111.
Woods, C. Stacey. "What Happens in Commitment?" Rev. of Edward John Carnell, Christian Commitment: An Apologetic (Macmillan). Eternity, March 1958, pp. 35-37.
Zehnal, Daniel J. "Irresponsible Evangelical," The Christian Century, Sept. 5, 1962, p. 1066.
Zetterholm, Earl E. Rev. of Edward John Carnell, Christian Commitment: An Apologetic (Macmillan). Westminster Theological Journal, May 1958, pp. 240-246.

www.ingramcontent.com/pod-product-compliance
Lightning Source LLC
Chambersburg PA
CBHW050803160426
43192CB00010B/1619